COMMON SIXTH SENSE

EXPANSION
HOUSE

UNLEASH YOUR MOST AUTHENTIC
CONNECTED LIFE

COMMON SIXTH SENSE

RACHAEL SCHMIDT

Published by  EXPANSION HOUSE

eBook ISBN: 979-8-9995335-2-4

Paperback ISBN: 979-8-9995335-0-0

Hardcover ISBN: 979-8-9995335-1-7

Library of Congress Control Number: 2025915138

First Edition

Book Production and Publishing by Brands Through Books

brandsthroughbooks.com

For my angels, August and Conner.

Live authentically and love yourself unconditionally.

NOTE TO READERS

As a mindfulness-based self-development educator and coach, I've dedicated the past twenty years to helping others awaken to their fullest potential through the integration of mindfulness, spiritual wisdom, and personal transformation—guiding them toward more connected, purposeful, and authentic lives.

If you're someone who craves deeper connection—to yourself, to others, and to life—this book was made for you.

Inside, you'll discover vignettes, practical tools, reflections, thought-provoking questions, and heartfelt stories—all designed to guide you toward a more authentic and connected way of living.

To truly get the most out of *Common Sixth Sense,* start at the beginning and give yourself the gift of time. Move through each page with curiosity and openness. Let the words settle in. Let them speak to you.

And when you reach the final page, don't stop there.

Keep this book close. Come back to it often.

Flip to a random page when you're feeling stuck.

Revisit a section that resonates with you.

Reflect on a question with fresh eyes.

This isn't a onetime read—it's a living, breathing resource meant to grow with you.

Dive in. Stay engaged. Let it challenge you, support you, and reconnect you. The more you interact with it, the more your own common sixth sense will awaken—and the more fully you'll step into the authentic and connected life you're meant to live.

CONTENTS

INTRODUCTION

IT IS TIME TO RETURN TO YOU.

COMMON SENSE IS NOT SO COMMON.
— VOLTAIRE

CHAPTER ONE

THE CRISIS

sixth sense
/siksTH 'sense

If common sense is not so common, imagine how much less common the understanding of the sixth sense must be. Yikes!

No one wants to be perceived as clueless about life or others. No one wants to be perceived as clueless about themselves. That's even worse.

Imagine how elevated your life could be if you understood your innate, intuitive language better. It is, after all, uniquely yours, so who better to understand it than you?

Move away from the idea that sixth sense abilities are only for psychics, mediums, empaths, and other intuitive or strongly connected people.

Move toward the idea that you already possess innate and intuitive abilities. Just because you haven't yet connected with these abilities or don't yet understand them doesn't mean they don't exist.

The goal is to engage with these abilities so you can finally access your most trusted advisor—you. This book will provide you with the rules of engagement to do so.

To understand your sixth sense, to have common sixth sense, is to simply understand yourself and your innate tools on a much deeper level and learn how to leverage this understanding to consistently lessen your suffering and improve your quality of life.

THE SIXTH SENSE

Let's break down the Oxford Dictionary definition.

"A supposed intuitive faculty giving awareness not explicable in terms of normal perception."

Supposed – Generally assumed or believed but not necessarily so.

Intuitive – Felt to be true with no evidence or proof.

Not explicable – Unable to be explained.

Normal perception – Vision, touch, sound, smell, taste, and proprioception (ability to sense movement).

In other words, people with a sixth sense connection feel and experience beyond "normal" perception.

Why would you ever want to be "normal" when you can access all of this?

Let's make sense of your sixth sense so you can start living your most authentic, connected life.

There is no better place to start than with spirituality. Think of your spirituality as a beacon of light inside of you, always shining and serving as a crucial navigational aid. Sometimes, we need to increase the brightness of our light to see more clearly. Are you ready to turn up your light?

SPIRITUALITY

You are a spiritual person. Period. You came like this.

When we hear the word *spirituality*, it conjures up all types of responses and opinions. For the sake of our work together, consider spirituality to be your sacred connection to yourself, to others, and to whatever it is you believe in that is bigger than yourself.

You need support, information, and tools to help you navigate your spirituality.

Spirituality exists within us all. The main challenge is learning how to set it free so you can truly experience "human" life as a connected, spiritual being.

We are getting too far removed from ourselves.

There is a connection crisis upon us. We have become too dependent on external resources to determine our happiness, peace, and understanding of self, and that is not good. As a matter of fact, it is concerningly, alarmingly, and holistically bad for you.

Why?

If you can think of a single reason why being disconnected from yourself would be beneficial to you, the people around you, or the world, please write it below.

_____

Notice the line remains blank.

Some of the most revered cultures in history had undeniably strong spiritual connections, represented through paintings, rituals, and symbolic archaeological findings and artifacts. The Incas and Aztecs even had sacrifices during powerful cosmic alignments.

Humanity has certainly recognized spirituality for quite some time. You would think we would be further along in our understanding of how to incorporate it into our lives in a healthy way by now. If it started this way—existing innately in people centuries ago—why are we still so confused about it? Nowadays, the term *spiritual* has become more mainstream, trendy even. Spiritual resources are readily available in the form of workshops, retreats, journals, and social media, but spirituality is so much deeper than what we are being sold on.

Recently, I was shopping for a journal for a friend and became overwhelmed by the large number of options. Bright covers, striped covers, journaling for anxiety, current mood journal, bucket list journal, and on and on. Lost at sea in clichés of "be brave" and "be the light," I opted for none of the above and went to get an iced green tea with agave at the on-site coffee shop instead. My quest to find the perfect gift reminded me that having too many resources often leads to analysis paralysis. My friend received an amber and fig candle instead.

I want to offer you a more simplified journey.

Many people seem stuck between two worlds—one where our authentic, connected, and spiritual self lives and another where we exist merely as a version of ourselves. This alternate world was constructed from a million pieces outside of ourselves. The entrapment of these two worlds leaves many people feeling like spiritual orphans—lost, without a mentor or guide, wandering aimlessly, looking everywhere for just one more piece of the puzzle, yet failing to realize this missing piece already exists inside of themselves.

Have you ever felt the conflict of these two worlds? Do you sense the opposing forces?

We all have moments when we feel lost and deprived.

We just want to find our way back home, where it is peaceful, supportive, and nurturing.

I am going to help guide you closer to home.

Let's get your feet wet by jumping right into the deep end. The deep end of the pool can be frightening, even petrifying for some, but once you get used to it, calm, peace, and serenity await you. Come jump into the deep end with me.

All you need is an open heart and an open mind.

We have reached a point where navigating life without a spiritual lens is too risky. We have so many external resources telling us how to live, what to think, and who we are. AI, technology, social media, and parental influence from childhood through adulthood can keep us too far removed from our authentic selves. If we don't prioritize our spiritual health now, it's just a matter of time before we get fully engulfed in the already suffocating influence of external resources. Good luck getting out then.

Start now.

There is not one specific type of spiritual person. As mentioned, we are all spiritual beings. Do not buy into the notion that spirituality is a defined construct. I have helped people navigate life through a spiritual lens for two decades, and nothing could be further from the truth. Spirituality lives within every type of person, representing all races, religions, identities, and demographics. My clients are a hodgepodge, a motley crew of humans ranging from teenagers to billionaires. I have educated young students in a classroom and the elderly in a senior living community. They have commonalities in that they are curious and want to explore mindfulness, spirituality, and connection on a deeper level, just like you may be doing now.

Does it feel like something is missing—and that if you had it, life would be, well . . . better or more peaceful? There is a very good chance it is your connection with self that you long for. Understanding how to navigate this connection and apply it to your life in meaningful ways can bring about an improved state of living.

We have all experienced connected moments. These memorable experiences may have lasted weeks, days, or even minutes. When you connect with yourself, it feels like a breath of air in between the two worlds, and if you keep exploring, eventually your inner voice emerges, takes control, and finally gets to replenish the oxygen it has been denied for far too long. We all need more of that.

To live your most connected life, you are going to need some common sixth sense. Your sixth sense is your greatest yet most underutilized asset. You just need clarity to understand how to effectively use the essential information it provides.

How authentically do you want to live in this life?

Many people have no idea who they are, although they will tell you they do. There are two groups of people. The first group is people who claim to know who they are but really don't want to find out. They are fine navigating life the way it is, even though it hurts themselves and others. They may even claim to be "enlightened" or "self-aware" but have not committed to the work, are not self-reflective, and typically (ironically) possess anything but self-awareness. The second group consists of those people who are curious and explorative and understand that the journey to knowing oneself is never-ending. You are most likely in the second group, ready for the infinite quest of self-connection.

The truth is that most people are not aware of the incredible tools they already possess that allow deep, spiritual connection with the self. This is not their fault. We only know what we know, right? You will know a lot more after reading this book, and I will be here as your personal guide, coach, and mentor from beginning to end.

That puzzle piece, that thing that is missing, the one you struggle to put into words, that longing—could it be a more connected life you are after?

What is on the other side of connection?

Peace. Understanding. Answers. Clarity.

Is your life a connected life?

Do you feel like something inside of you is trying to get out?

You have two lives: the life you are living and the authentic, unlived life inside of you.

You are doing a disservice to yourself and those around you if you only live one life.

When you establish a strong connection with your inner voice, you unleash the authentic, unlived life inside of you.

In my spiritual- and mindfulness-based coaching practice, most people I have worked with have very similar motivations.

1. To find more consistent peace
2. To learn how to trust their inner voice
3. To learn how to trust something bigger than themselves
4. To obtain tools to unleash the unlived life inside their soul

You must participate if you want to experience a more connected life. Spirituality and connection are not something reserved for a Tuesday or when you are in the mood. It's a lifestyle. Your authentic voice aches to be heard and is eager to lead. Are you willing to finally give this voice the acknowledgment and attention it deserves? The more you create a life where you tap into yourself, the more connected living will become part of your daily life—a lifestyle. Try moving away from the idea that spirituality is something you do and let it become who you are. Try moving away from the idea that connection is an infrequent occurrence and let it become a common experience in everyday life.

Okay, but how?

This book will take you on a unique exploration that will lead you closer to your answer—not anyone else's answer. Remember, the answer is personalized to the individual. Your specific how is the result of your self-exploration, where you and only you can uncover your secret sauce, your method, your code, your algorithm, and your magic formula that allows you to experience a more connected life.

Self-connection does not need to be overly complicated. Yes, it is deep and soulful and cathartic, but you do not always have to travel long distances to get there. Life can be a cross-country trek through treacherous lands with much trial and error, but I hope to shorten the trip a bit for you by sharing pieces of my algorithm and the successful tools that have impacted the wonderful souls I have been blessed to coach and guide for the past twenty years. What I have discovered is that simplified concepts, thought-provoking questions, and daily tools can have a big impact on quality of life and well-being.

May this book be the shortest return trip home—to you.

Now that you have gotten your feet wet, let's dive deeper. Come back to my childhood with me.

CHAPTER TWO

THE CHALLENGE

All I can think about is diving into the deep end of the pool. The blue abyss, with sacred healing powers, never disappoints. The bottom of the pool is my salvation, so quiet and centering. The way the sun reflects creates multiple blurred, white lines. I could live here, but the whistle from above tells me I should retreat, for now. I reluctantly exit the water, but I won't go far from the edge of the pool. I can be closer when the whistle blows again. The waiting feels like forever, and my skin is now dry from the mixture of sunshine and chlorine. Finally, the whistle comes again, and permission is granted. I gracefully collide with the water. Everything feels so smooth, so perfect, so peaceful.

Was there a time in your childhood when you felt utterly connected, at peace, and completely in line with who you are?

Then . . . life rips us away from ourselves. It could be a trauma, a circumstance, something someone said or did or did not say or do, or something we said or did or did not say or do. Next comes the energy shift away from the way we were before the incident, or the words, or the circumstance. We were free-spirited in the moment of watching the sun reflect on top of the water. Now, we are still us, but we are a somewhat divided version of ourselves. For many, it has been a long time since we watched the sun reflect on top of the water—too long. The goal is to reclaim our absolute authenticity—if not completely, then to get as damn close as we can.

But you must be more mindful.

Why the focus on mindfulness?

Mindfulness is the ability to stay present without judgment. To be mindful is to notice something you previously did not notice, to become aware of what was previously outside your awareness.

When was the last time you did that?

When we are in the present moment (mindful, noticing), our minds, bodies, and spirits feel aligned.

You may have heard the expression "be here now."

The deeper you go into this book, the more I encourage you to stay present, to be here now, and notice something you had not previously noticed, especially when it comes to yourself. Give yourself permission to put responsibilities on hold while you mindfully read the pages of this book. You need and deserve this time to strengthen the relationship with yourself.

The more present you are in your life, the more valuable your life experiences become.

If you have ever been fully engrossed in a conversation, a workout, observing an object, sitting quietly by yourself, petting your dog, or enjoying the warm sun on your face, chances are you were mindfully connected in those moments. You were presently aware, and there is nothing quite like experiencing the present moment.

So much of mindfulness is about awareness (noticing), and that is why it is a vital foundation for connection.

Here is another definition of mindfulness to consider: Keep your mind on what is right in front of you and simply notice.

Distraction is the opposite of mindfulness.

Does being mindful actually benefit us?

What about the science behind mindfulness?

Mindfulness is supported by a large and growing body of scientific evidence. The benefits of mindfulness-based practices, such as meditation, have been extensively researched. For further exploration into the science of mindfulness, consider the past and ongoing work of Dr. Jon Kabat-Zinn of the University of Massachusetts Medical School. As the pioneer of the Mindfulness-Based Stress Reduction (MBSR) program, Dr. Kabat-Zinn has been at the forefront of mindfulness research since the 1980s. His studies have demonstrated reductions in stress, anxiety, and depression and have even shown changes in brain and immune function as a result of meditation practices (Kabat-Zinn, 2015).

Other notable researchers include Dr. Ellen Langer, a social psychologist and professor at Harvard University, who has studied mindfulness for over forty years with a focus on aging, perspective, and happiness (Langer, 1991). Dr. Richard Davidson, a neuroscientist at the University of Wisconsin–Madison, has conducted research on mindfulness and positive mental health outcomes (Treves et al., 2025). Dr. Marsha Linehan, professor emeritus at the University of Washington, has advanced mindfulness as a clinical treatment intervention (Dimidjian & Linehan, 2003). Dr. Amishi Jha, a cognitive neuroscientist at the University of Miami, explores the neuroscience of attention and mindfulness (Gunsilius et al., 2024). Dr. Christopher Germer, along with Dr. Kristin Neff, has contributed significantly to research on mindful self-compassion in psychotherapy (Neff & Germer, 2013).

Additional influential researchers include Dr. Ruth Baer, who has studied outcomes of mindfulness-based interventions (Chems-Maarif et al., 2025), and Dr. Kirk Warren Brown of Carnegie Mellon University, whose work emphasizes the importance of awareness (Brown, Crewell & Ryan, 2025). Collectively, these researchers have deepened our understanding of how mindfulness affects brain function, cognition, and emotional well-being.

So, yes, mindfulness benefits us.

We get our teeth cleaned at the dentist and get yearly mammograms or annual blood work as preventative health measures. Why do we do all of this? The research tells us that if we take preventative measures, we can prevent or decrease the risk of suffering.

Think of mindfulness as a preventative tool—not as something you do when it's too late but as something you do to prevent and manage suffering.

MINDFULNESS = AWARENESS (NOTICING) = SELF-AWARENESS

Mindfulness is a foundation for developing your common sixth sense.

Do not wait for fleeting experiences. Connect today, tonight, right now. This is what mindfulness is all about—the here and now.

When we reflect on our connected moments, they typically stand out. Perhaps it was a celebratory event or concert where the energy in the room ignited you. Perhaps it was an intimate conversation where you felt safe enough to be vulnerable without self-judgment. What about having a nonverbal exchange with a stranger, watering a plant, taking a walk, feeling a cool breeze on your face, or even sitting alone without an agenda? The truth is all moments, even the mundane ones, are opportunities for connection.

If you want to experience more frequent connections, you must participate. Remember, the goal is to shift the power away from external influences and return it to where it belongs—with you. You cannot experience a shift in your life unless you take action, and this requires your proactive participation.

Every time you gain more awareness, you receive valuable information needed to take action. This action creates the space needed for the shift to occur. The more you shift, the more power you claim.

How much do you rely on external resources, such as your partner, friends, family, or work colleagues, to provide connection? We all have expectations of others—how they should respond, act, think, and so on. We are often left confused as to why people are incapable of connecting in the way we need to connect. This is normal human behavior. But remember, why would you want to be normal when you could be so much more?

How much are you directly contributing to the connections you need in your life versus passively relying on others to provide them? To what extent do you understand the connections you need? Are the connections you seek superficial, due to anxious attachment, or simply out of habit?

Your common sixth sense will help you more clearly define healthy and aligned connections.

Why do we even seek deeper connections anyway? Here are a few reasons.

Lack of Quality Connections

We may feel a void with current relationships and environments and ache for elevated experiences.

To Explore Deep, Existential Questions

We are curious by nature and seek like-minded people and thought-provoking resources to support us as we dive into our deep end.

For Peace

We all need more peace. Our bodies, minds, and spirits are not designed for chronic stress and suffering. Human beings are resilient and have endured so much, and we can agree that the human mind, body, and spirit have remarkable survival skills. However, if you have experienced chronic stress and suffering, you have all the data you need to know with absolute certainty that we are not designed for this state of being.

To Be Understood

We do not want to experience life alone. No matter how much you proclaim you do not need anyone and can get through life all on your own, you are doing a disservice to yourself by refusing what others have to offer and the camaraderie and connection that result from receiving support and shared experiences.

For Alignment

We are intuitively trying to bridge the gap between our spiritual self and the outside world. This is a constant energy struggle. Connection helps us build that bridge one layer at a time. Think of connection like a chiropractic adjustment. Ahh, that feels amazing!

Perhaps those who are skeptical about their intuition and innate abilities contribute to the energy struggle. The skepticism itself is counterintuitive. If you do not believe you can utilize the natural resources you came with or that they even exist, it is understandable that you may feel misaligned and struggle with connection.

Which reason above resonates with you most in your life now? Does your inner world feel like a match or a mismatch with the outside world? What words describe this mismatch for you?

Let's dive deeper.

- Do you use an umbrella when it rains?
- Do you look both ways before crossing the street?
- Do you wear a seat belt?
- Do you ask for help when you need it?
- Do you apologize when you have made a mistake?
- Do you wear sunscreen?
- Do you keep hazardous chemicals away from small children and pets?

If most of your answers are a resounding yes, you are using common sense. Congratulations!

Now, what about your sixth sense?

- Do you listen to your gut feelings?
- Do you pay attention to synchronicity?
- Do you avoid danger?
- Do you pick up on hidden emotions in others?
- Do you recognize opportunities others overlook?
- Do you pick up on subtle changes?
- Do you sense the right moment to do or say something?
- Do you feel like some things are meant to be?
- Do you show empathy to others?

If some of your answers are yes, you have collaborated with your sixth sense. Remember, your sixth sense is your most valuable yet most underutilized asset. Why would you refuse directions from your most skilled navigator?

When you apply your common sixth sense abilities and start working as a team, you will experience shifts in your life that allow this incredible partnership to blossom and the authentic self to emerge. Together, you can create your most connected life.

It takes time, practice, and energy to understand your innate abilities. It does not matter where you are now; it only matters where you are headed. If you are feeling too far removed from all of this, please, do not worry. Your spirit is patient, kind, and understanding. A reunion is always an option at any time. Keep reading. This book is for everyone and anyone who wants to live a more connected life, even if you do not use sunscreen or pick up on the hidden emotions of others. (You really should wear sunscreen, though.)

Do not forget that you are a human being, and human beings are, well, human. It is impossible to feel connected all the time. Do not set unrealistic expectations for your life. Allow yourself the human experience you have been gifted. This is why applying your common sixth sense is imperative—so you can find more peace in your humanness so you can just be.

Your connectedness is always available to you, but sometimes, when we get hyperfixated on connection, we disconnect. It's okay to disconnect sometimes.

What is the driving force that has propelled you to pick up this book?

A – Desire for connection

B – Self-exploration

C – Spiritual expansion

D – All of the above

Something else entirely? Write it below.

_____

Are you ready for a challenge?

Do you accept the challenge to become a proactive participant in your most connected life?

It will not happen by accident. It only happens with your involvement.

Where do you begin? With breathing. Take a big, deep breath.

CHAPTER THREE

THE BREATH

While lying in a hospital bed, awaiting surgery at UCLA Medical Center, I was struck by a ferocious wave that delivered a powerful and concise message. This wave jolted me while simultaneously delivering a claircognizant (clear knowing) message that everything would be all right. I experienced a sense of calm and serenity I had never felt before. I understood this wave to be an awareness, a gift of clarity delivered by something much bigger than myself. Upon receiving this message, I became hyperaware of my breath, almost like the breath itself spoke to me and said, "Just breathe." This voice allowed me one of the most peaceful moments I have experienced in my life.

My euphoria was quickly altered when the nurse appeared and offered medication for my apparent surgery anxiety, which ironically, was perfectly timed to the moment she entered the room. My newfound clarity dissipated as I surrendered to my medicated state of relaxation. I knew the outcome was in God's hands, but I quickly reminded myself I was in the city of angels anyway. As I eased deeper into sleep, however hard I tried, I could not fight off the fearful voice demanding to know How the hell did I get here? Will I get out alive? Sets of eyes over masked faces looked over me, and I could tell they were smiling by the deep creases at the corners. These smiles did offer a last bit of comfort before they performed the craniotomy.

I groggily awoke to my fatigued yet relieved husband, who never looked more handsome, like the month of September in a calendar, wearing scrubs and holding a stuffed animal and flowers. I rejoiced by raising a couple of fingers and grunting to confirm I somehow survived the brain surgery. I'd been diagnosed with a rare vestibular disorder called superior semicircular canal dehiscence (SSCD), a rather insidious condition where the bone separating the brain and circular ear canal is weak and filled with holes, in my case. The result was a third ear window that wreaked havoc on my vestibular system. I experienced dizziness fifty times a day, could hear my own heartbeat, experienced sound-induced vertigo, and lived in absolute misery. But an outsider would have never known. SSCD is a silent disorder. I looked normal and healthy; however, on the inside, there was a heavy metal concert I would never buy tickets to and a tornado of suffering—unpredictable, chaotic, and unstoppable.

Ten days after the surgery, I got the green light to head home. After my full security pat down at LAX, which took every ounce of energy from my body, my husband pushed my wheelchair through the crowded airport, its wheels squeaking and wobbling at every turn. Finally, we arrived at the gate. I remember making eye contact with a few travelers before early boarding. They looked at me with eyes wide open and stretched out necks, indicating they were empathetic to my current state. I appreciated the nonverbal empathy but despised the fact that they assumed I was incapable or on my deathbed. I boarded that flight and headed home to reclaim my life.

I survived one nightmare but still had work ahead of me. Much about the condition remains unknown, and the postoperative plan was unclear, as my doctors disagreed on the specific next steps. I quickly realized I was on my own. After eight years, fifteen doctors—including specialists at Mayo Clinic and University of Miami Health, and nearly every neuro and ENT expert in South Florida—and one experimental procedure in Fort Worth, Texas, I now wear my hearing aids with pride. They're a byproduct of the surgery-related hearing loss that once left me mortified at the thought of needing them. Now, I finally feel back in my body—more or less. It's a different world inside this body, but still, I'm grateful.

I've always valued the breath—from diving into glistening water as a swimmer to moving through Vinyasa yoga, navigating parenting, sitting in Florida traffic, or managing everyday chaos. Yet, even with this deep appreciation, I underestimated the breath's power during my darkest moments. The breath is a powerhouse sixth sense tool, and it seems like my breath always has my back.

After letting my dogs out at 10:00 p.m. on a thirty-four-degree night in Texas in November, as I stood on my backyard patio, I was confronted by a man in a mask, wearing surgical gloves and holding a gun. I ran to an upstairs closet, hitting the alarm system's panic button along the way. On the phone with 911, in that closet filled with winter jackets and boxes of random knickknacks, I contemplated the possibility of my last breath. The wave hit once again, only this time, it was familiar. The overwhelming sense of serenity engulfed me. I remembered this wave, the one I'd had before my surgery at UCLA just one year earlier. I was briskly transported from panic to peace as I repeated once again, "Just breathe, breathe, breathe."

This event ignited a two-and-a-half-year criminal case during COVID that ended with more questions than answers and the guilty party fleeing the country two days before his six-month jail sentence was to begin.

My mind, body, and spirit were relentlessly jolted. Life felt chaotic and unpredictable. I was tired, in survival mode, and I wanted out.

I made the decision that, despite what I had experienced, I would take full responsibility for creating my most connected and authentic life.

I had to relearn how to connect to myself and my life again without excessive anxiety and fear, while juggling parenting and the daily chronic stress of my vestibular disorder.

There was immense benefit from the breath during these traumatic experiences. My understanding of applying the breath as a tool to get closer to a more connected life became clear, obvious even, and I credit these events for the evolution of the common sixth sense concepts. These experiences expanded my appreciation of the breath.

The breath, your breath, is so valuable.

Let's just start there.

Take a breath.

Your breath is a powerful common sixth sense resource.

Besides the obvious things we all need to heal, like time, support, and self-compassion, what ultimately alleviated my suffering was a conversation with one of my graduate-level criminal justice students in the mindfulness integration course I was teaching. This student worked at the county jail and was a no-nonsense type who did not mince words. I was telling her about the case and my victim impact statement when she interrupted me and stated, "They don't care. Some criminals just don't care." It was not rude; it was the truth. In that moment, we had intense eye contact, and I took a deep breath (there it was again), felt a spiritual shift, and let out a psychological sigh. Sometimes, it's that simple to end suffering—taking a big, deep breath, accepting reality, and deciding what energy you want to continue to exert.

Why continue wasting energy and breath on ruminating, relentless questioning, and seeking answers that may never be found?

Consider something in your life you have relentlessly struggled to understand. How does it feel to imagine you may never have an answer?

Sometimes, reality and breath are the best of friends.

A truth can set you free, and a breath can confirm that you have, in fact, accepted the truth.

A breath can give you the freedom you need in the most unexpected of times. A breath is the deepest release from suffering. Pay attention to your breath. Use your common sixth sense.

In both situations—the surgery and home break-in—there were and still are so many unanswered questions. I had to find peace with both to live my most connected and authentic life.

The only place you can find peace is within. It is in the surrender that we find peace, and the surrender can only come from you.

You know what helps us surrender? The breath.

I was searching, sometimes obsessively and desperately, for answers. How can I feel 100 percent back to myself? There must be one more doctor who can figure this out! Why was this man at my house, trying to get in for over an hour? What was he going to do with the duct tape in his backpack? Even overflowing piles of accumulated medical documents and conversations with the district attorney did not produce many answers. There was certainly a cumulative effect from outside sources that lightened the weight and allowed me some sanity along the way, but there was not an MD or DA who could have done what I could only do for myself. I had to figure out my formula to shift from surviving to thriving.

I never considered myself a victim, but still, I felt my peace had been stolen, and I wanted it back.

Have you ever felt like your peace has been stolen?

Always keep an unstoppable drive when it comes to your quality of life. Remember, you are your best advocate. No matter what has happened to you or what you will endure in the future, never stop pursuing your most authentic and connected life.

It was largely through my understanding and appreciation for the breath that I have been able to maintain a positive perspective throughout the unexpected events of my life. As a matter of fact, the breath was so relevant and comforting for me in my dark moment that I had to ask my breath, "Did we just become best friends?"

There is so much power in the breath. It is one of your most critical and most underutilized innate tools. Having a more solid understanding of the power of your breath can change your life.

The breath is your first step whenever you feel disconnected on any level—whether you're sitting in traffic, calming yourself after an intense moment, or preparing for whatever comes next. Just breathe.

Start using your breath.

You take roughly twenty thousand breaths per day (Stephen, 2021). How many of those twenty thousand breaths are you even aware of?

Take a deep breath.

Take another.

And another.

Ah, now you are becoming more aware.

Always, always (and I mean always) start with the breath.

Think about what is weighing the most heavily on you right now.

Take a breath.

That is all you need to do for now.

You won't believe how much you can expand your awareness by simply taking a few breaths.

CHAPTER FOUR

THE AWARENESS

If you can manage your energy, you can manage your life.

If you want to unlock your formula for energy freedom, you must discover your code. You are the only one who can understand the cipher.

I will share some of my code, but you must uncover your own. It's the only way.

Why do we even want to manage energy? It is simple: to reduce suffering.

People waste so much energy trying to manage other people's energy instead of their own. You cannot manage other people's energy, but you can inspire them with your own energy management system.

How much of your energy are you giving away to others? Too much? Do you even want to give your energy away? Just because you are mindlessly giving your energy away does not mean you genuinely want to or that it benefits your quality of life in any way.

What people are you allowing to use up your energy? Which people stand out most when you think of expelling a lot of your energy? What percentage of your energy do you think you deplete on these people? What amount of your energy are you typically distributing to them? How do you feel after giving these people your energy? Are you mindlessly giving it away for free? Contemplate if you even want to give them that much energy in the first place. Be honest.

And what about you? What percentage of your energy do you allocate to yourself? Are you getting enough of your energy? Are there people who deserve more of your energy?

Everything is energy. When you interact with people, you are experiencing an energy exchange.

Energy is positive. Energy is negative. Energy is neutral.

Energy holds power—chemical, mechanical, nuclear, and beyond. I'll skip the technical details for now. Just know energy is everything and is everywhere.

People are energy. Your experience with people is dependent upon your energy management skills. How do you think you respond to energy? Consider asking the people around you for perspective. Hmm, now it is getting interesting.

Does the way you believe you manage energy align with how others perceive your energy management? What if it does not align? Is it possible you are mismanaging your energy?

Reflect for a moment, please. Contemplate a recent situation that demonstrates your mismanagement of energy. Now, contemplate a recent situation that demonstrates your healthy energy management. See the difference?

Our energy management impacts our lens of life—how we see ourselves, others, and the world. Ideally, we want to experience life with a wide-angle lens to capture what exists beyond normal perception.

THE LENS OF LIFE

To experience your most connected life, you need to understand the lens of life.

Lens of Life Scale

Some people have very wide life lenses.

Others, not so much.

Some lenses are so narrow, you may need reading glasses or a magnifying glass to see them.

If you have ever been around a narrow-lens individual, you know they resist perspectives or opinions that are not in alignment with their own. Perhaps not much has changed or evolved within them or their life for quite some time. Self-awareness is not a strength of theirs, and your time with them is nothing short of uninspiring or unsettling. It typically leaves you feeling fatigued or in an energy conflict with them, whether they know it or not.

It is an energy drain to interact with a narrow-lens person, especially if you are a wide-lens person. You know who loves narrow-lens people? Other narrow-lens people.

What narrow-lens people in your life disrupt your energy? Is it Ron from accounting? I know, he is super annoying. How about a dysfunctional family member? The negative friend who complains incessantly? The off-putting parking attendant you interact with daily, who, after you say, "Good morning," responds with a growl? We cannot always hide from narrow-lens people, but we can learn to manage our energy interactions with them.

How wide is your lens? It does not matter what size it is today. Know you have everything you need within you to continue widening your lens.

Some people have narrow lenses. It is not your job to widen their lens; however, it is your responsibility to keep widening your own lens.

If someone has a narrow lens, accept this truth. Whenever you catch yourself feeling responsible for—or determined to expand—another person's lens, pause and take a deep breath. This will no doubt spare you from anger, frustration, and even suffering. It's their lens, not yours. You will waste exorbitant amounts of energy attempting to widen the lens of a rigid, stubborn, narrow-lens person.

Have you ever been in an unhealthy relationship or friendship where you convinced yourself the other person could change? Perhaps you have taken on the self-appointed role of the fixer? Yep, it's like that.

You cannot determine the outcome of your influence on their lens, but you can inspire them with your own energy management.

How much of your precious, sacred energy do you want to keep mindlessly giving away? Why would you give your energy away mindlessly when you can mindfully manage it?

When you cross paths with a narrow-lens person, you must:

1. Anticipate – Take protective measures before interacting.
2. Be realistic – You have been here before and certainly know how this will play out for you.
3. Regulate your sense of giving – Set boundaries. Commit to the amount of energy you plan to exert and honor the agreement you make with yourself.

The healthiest course of action is that which protects your vital energy.

Much of your struggle is believing other people should share your same lens on life, but only you can see clearly through your lens.

We spend way too much energy trying to widen other people's lenses. Focus on your lens.

How open is your mind?

Draw it below.

What does it look like? Is it colorful? Is it expansive? Perhaps today, in this moment, it feels blocked. Use your intuition to guide you. Do not overthink it; just draw.

For perspective, come back in one year, after your common sixth sense skills have evolved, and draw your mind again below.

Can you find comfort in the uncomfortable? I hope so because life is uncomfortable. We deal with discomfort all the time. Luckily, discomfort is an alarm that alerts you when something is off. There are, of course, many layers of discomfort, ranging from experiencing numb fingertips while shoveling snow to speaking in front of others or feeling gutted as you hold the collar of a recently lost and beloved pet.

How do we find comfort in the uncomfortable? By breathing.

Your knowledge of this common sixth sense skill is growing. Always breathe first. Discomfort, breath. Discomfort, breath. You get the idea.

Your breath will always comfort you.

When you breathe, you are exchanging oxygen and carbon dioxide in the body. Your breath activates the parasympathetic nervous system, which sends a signal to your brain, telling you that you are safe.

But so much more is happening. You are reducing tension, slowing your heart rate, improving blood flow, and increasing oxygen.

The breath returns you to you, which is exactly where you belong. This is your home. The breath has so much power. We take our first breath and our last breath, and in between these breaths, we are trying to figure out how to live the best damn life we can.

If something has this much power and you have access to it, why are you not using it to your full advantage?

Let's do a quick recap.

Spirituality + Mindfulness + Energy Management = A More Connected Life

Throw in the power of the breath, awareness, and an understanding of the lens of life. Whoa! Now you're cooking!

Remember, as your awareness increases, so does your self-awareness.

Are you becoming more aware now?

How self-aware are you?

Question: How can we tell how self-aware someone is?

Answer: From the actions one takes or does not take based on information obtained from being aware.

Awareness = Self-Awareness

Awareness is one thing, but *action* is everything.

Let's go to seventh-century BC Greece.

The Greeks built a majestic temple to honor the god Apollo at Delphi. Apollo was the god of healing, light, the sun, and the arts, to name a few of his domains.

There was an inscription on top of the temple with the following words:
Γνῶθι σεαυτόν
Gnōthi Seauton

Do you know what this inscription says? Bonus points if you can say it in Greek.

It says, "Know Thyself."

Know thyself has been interpreted by so many, from Socrates to Plato, but it seems the meaning is self-explanatory.

Do you think the Greeks who painstakingly built this temple are hanging out with Apollo, looking down on all of us and screaming, "We already gave you the answer! The answer is know thyself, people! It's know thyself!"

They must be so frustrated with us.
So . . . how well do you know thyself?
Take a minute to think about it.

You may have felt a slight jolt or a little uncomfortable when I asked you how well you know thyself.
If you did, that is energy.

It does not necessarily matter how well you know yourself at this time in your life; it only matters that you are willing to learn and expand the relationship.
Are you willing?

CHAPTER FIVE

THE FORMULA

Where there is a will, there is a way.

In my mindfulness-based self-development business, many of my clients come to me with fear, frustration, and feelings of disconnection and loneliness. They desire a shift. They are willing participants but need clarity. The majority are high-functioning and, from the outside looking in, appear to be doing just fine—but inside, something feels off, like it's trying to find its way out.

Have you ever been forced to open your bulging luggage at the airport because it exceeded the fifty-pound limit, or sat down with a longtime friend only to realize you no longer have much in common? On a deeper level, it feels like your soul is an XL, and your body is a size two.

Something is not fitting right.

But do not worry. Will is essential for making the decision to initiate action—and you have will. Your unwavering willpower, combined with faith and the tools in this book, will get you to a place of reconnection.

Being aware that there is a disconnect or a desire for more is good. No, it's not just good—it is excellent!

Awareness first, then self-connection.

The goal is to create a more connected life, one where connection is common, a part of everyday living.

How?

Let's start with something simple.

$$E = mc^2$$

This is Einstein's theory of relativity. Einstein understood the profound power of energy. The theory of relativity is a complex principle that took roughly seven years to develop. I do not want you to spend the next seven years painstakingly developing a formula.

I am going to simplify energy for you. I call it the *theory of volatility*.

How volatile are you when impacted by energy?

E
Energy

M
My management (or mismanagement) of energy

C
Chaos

C
Calm

$E = mc^2$
Energy, including my own, other people's, environments, technology, etc.

=

My chaos or *my* calm

How you manage (or mismanage) energy = your chaos or your calm

It is that simple.

Well-managed energy = calm

Poorly managed energy = chaos

Well-managed energy benefits you and everything and everyone you interact with. Poorly managed energy is a disservice to you and everything and everyone you interact with.

SENSATIONS—THE GREAT COMMUNICATORS

We have all been in situations where we have felt visceral responses, intense inward feelings not originating from intellect.

These sensations are the greatest communicators. They can literally save your life. "I just knew not to turn down the street before the accident occurred." We have all heard these stories, or perhaps you have experienced a profound "divine intervention" of your own. The retelling of these experiences usually begins with, "Something did not feel right" or "Something overcame me."

Perhaps it is difficult for you to describe, best explained as a sensation that vibrates throughout you. These sensations feel intuitive, although you may be unable to determine the point of origin. This is the energy of your intuition, your inner voice communicating to you on your behalf. It is quite literally you communicating with you.

This visceral communication—these sensations—can not only intervene in life-threatening situations by steering you away from the "bad" but also guide you in daily life toward the "good" and, ultimately, back to your authentic self. These sensations are there to tell you what is right as much as what is wrong. They are typically undeniable and intense for a reason—so you will pay attention and listen.

Never deny, dismiss, or explain away your visceral sensations. They are to be acknowledged, honored, and respected. When we discredit these sensations, there is a significant energy risk. When we ignore valuable alerts about ourselves, others, or the world, it can certainly impact our energy. The information provided by our visceral sensations is invaluable. You have a built-in notification system for survival, safety, health, and emotional well-being. Why would you dismiss it? Come on, you have some common sixth sense now.

When friction, separation, and induction cause static electricity, you get a zap, a jolt—blatant, undeniable, and commonly referred to as a shock. Sometimes, while folding laundry or touching a doorknob, you feel that unexpected energy surge, causing a disruption.

This disruption alerts you, saying, "Hey, this does not work!" Think oil and water, fire and ice, or wearing a white shirt while eating pasta with marinara sauce. This is why we must be extra careful when pumping gas. Gasoline and static electricity do not vibe well. Boom! Pay attention to your energy disruptions because they are working on your behalf.

Jolts can be alarming—sometimes loud and blaring, other times soft and subtle—but they are always present. We have minor and major jolts and apathetically ignore them. Every. Single. Day.

If someone forgets to use a turn signal in traffic, you may feel jolted. If your mom reminds you one more time, or your spouse gives you the look, yep, that is a jolt all right.

The most impactful jolts cut way deeper, and we initiate most of them ourselves. We judgmentally examine our bodies in the mirror, reaching all sorts of outlandish conclusions. We overthink about a mistake we made years ago, abuse ourselves with drugs and alcohol, repeatedly participate in people-pleasing behaviors that leave us short on energy, ignore symptomatic health issues, and neglect stress management. Those jolts cut really deep. We are highly skilled at self-inflicted jolts.

There is a huge spectrum of jolts, but they all have value. All jolts have value because all jolts deliver important messages.

As the saying goes, don't kill the messenger. The jolt is not your enemy; it just delivers the message. Intense, sometimes unpleasant jolts can deliver the most profound information. Think of the jolt like that friend who always says what they think, does not sugarcoat, and gives you valuable, honest advice—and yes, that stings sometimes, but it gets your attention.

Lean into the jolts and be curious about the messages. Messages are catalysts for growth. When we get jolted, we have two choices: react or take purposeful action. If we simply react to a jolt, we are disconnected. If we take purposeful action, we experience connection.

It is impossible to always take purposeful action. Sometimes, we react because we are human beings, and environments or people get the best of us. Give yourself some grace in these types of situations, apologize to others or yourself if warranted, and move on.

The goal is to have more connection than disconnection. To do so, you must take purposeful action.

What is the first step after you receive a jolt?

STEP 1

Breathe

A jolt often feels like we are removed from our body. We feel outside of ourselves. That feeling is an energy surge.

Think of a gong being struck and the vibrations moving in and out of you, momentarily pulling you away from yourself.

When jolted, it can feel like we exit ourselves.

Perhaps you have your own unique way to describe your jolts. What does a jolt feel like to you?

What are we going to do with all that energy surging through us? First, we breathe, and then we must transfer the energy.

STEP 2

The Transfer

We do not want to keep the energy inside—it will do all sorts of damage—so it must go somewhere else.

Where? Anywhere, just as long as it does not stay inside of you.

Personally, I visualize an energy surge traveling down my legs, through my feet, and into the earth. I imagine thick tree roots carrying all that energy far away from me. I have clients who like to visualize the energy traveling through the tops of their heads, into the sky, and exploding in space. Some of my clients visualize their inner energy flowing like an air filter, working on their behalf to clear out negativity.

Try touching an object and passing the energy through your hand. Try visualizing a beautiful white light engulfing your body. Keep experimenting with your energy transfer. It does not matter how you do it; it only matters that it works for you. Make it your own.

Now, you are starting to create your secret formula for your most connected life.

With your breath and your energy transfer working together as a solid team, you initiate the return to your body. Ahh, there you are.

STEP 3

The Return

Welcome back to you.

STEP 4

The Decision

You have a decision to make. As long as the decision supports your well-being, it is the right decision.

We will go much more in depth with the decision later.

After you make your decision, you must act.

STEP 5

The Action

A decision does not exist without action.

Doing nothing is an action if it is made consciously and is not simply the result of a reaction.

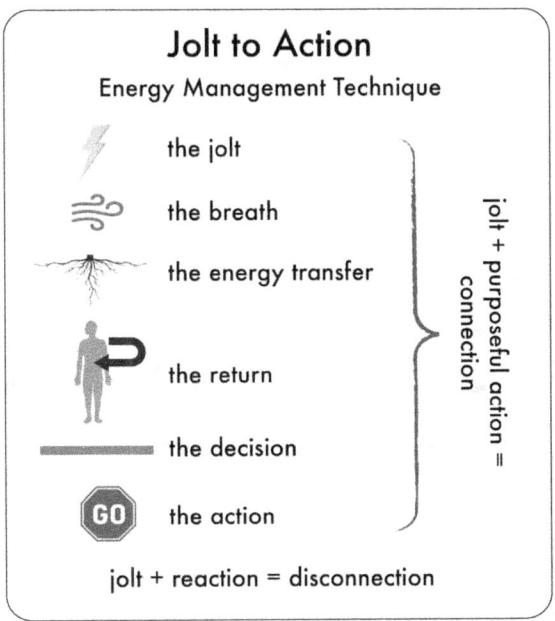

If you react, you are disconnected. If you take purposeful action, you experience connection. They have significantly different outcomes. One outcome reduces your suffering; the other does not.

Awareness is one thing, but action is everything.

If you can master your energy, you can master your life.
Let that sink in.

Incorporating the foundations for your common sixth sense into your daily life can bring you so much closer to you.

- Spirituality
- Mindfulness
- Energy management

With these foundations in place, you will be a triple threat. Can you imagine the life you can create with these foundations integrated into your lifestyle? If you want to align your inner world with your outer world, you must gain clarity on the three foundations and bring that clarity into your life.

THE AIR PURIFIER

An air purifier improves the quality of the air we breathe by continually and consistently reducing allergens, viruses, pollutants, and contaminants through a purification process. The purification process is impossible without the most vital piece: the filter. Have you ever changed out an air filter that was long overdue? It is quite unsettling to see what has accumulated. Not only does this leave behind a filthy, dusty mess of unidentifiable debris, but it also restricts any current or future purification, halting the entire process.

Consider the negative energy you encounter every day from people, environments, circumstances, and technology. Your body, mind, and spirit must purify this energy. Take one good look at that dirty air filter because that is all you need to understand what can happen inside of yourself if you do not keep your filter clean continually and consistently. We must keep a committed filter replacement schedule to ensure the purest, highest quality of air.

I would prefer to have as much clean energy in my mind, body, and spirit as possible. What about you?

However, that will not happen if you are a passive receiver of energy. You must be a proactive participant in your filtration system.

If we do not filter negative energy, everyone loses. People say, "I don't care," "I am not bothered by it," or "It's fine," yet they continue to talk about it, complain, relive it, and frantically seek out anyone willing to listen as they retell every detail of the thing they supposedly don't care about. Do you know anyone like this? You can run from energy vampires, but you cannot hide, and they are out for your blood. How does it affect you when you interact with this type of energy? Do you see how poor filtration is projected onto others?

I know you would never behave like this—completely lacking self-awareness—because you are gaining common sixth sense.

A compelling story deserves to be retold, but the people who struggle to filter negative energy are typically not telling the most compelling stories.

You must filter continually and consistently. For optimal functioning, negative energy must be filtered. You are literally the filtration system.

The Air Purifier

Take in energy that resonates and filter out the rest. Have the courage to prioritize, respect, and honor your filter. Do not be a passive consumer of negative energy. Everyone benefits from your ability to filter.

YOUR PERCEPTION = YOUR REALITY

Whatever you focus on gets amplified. However you perceive your life, you are turning the volume up on that perception.

Is the perception of your life like that one incredible song you absolutely love, the one that never gets old, no matter how many times you hear it?

Personally, I like to crank up the volume on a song I love and dance like no one is watching.

What do you want to turn the volume up on? What do you want to turn the volume down on?

However you perceive your life is the life you live and the song you play on repeat.

No matter what has happened in your life, you deserve to live an authentic and connected life. You deserve a song you love.

Your life has purpose. Your life is an opportunity. Every day presents you with the choice to shift your perception.

Do not wait for something good to happen. Do not wait for someone. Do not wait until tomorrow. Start shifting now.

How? By practicing gratitude.

Start with a moment. That's all. Acknowledge and appreciate the breath inside of you. Allow it to expand and deepen. Build upon the appreciation. Start the day thankful. You didn't *make it* another day; you *get* another day.

You will naturally begin to recognize all the beauty you have ignored in yourself, in your environment, and in others.

Open your eyes to what is versus what is not. Lessen your focus on changing things and people. Shift your desires away from "if only" and toward today.

It's okay to want more, but what you have and who you are is certainly enough to be thankful for today.

Gratitude not only reduces your suffering but also elevates your perception and enhances your reality. With gratitude on your side, you are better able to manage the voices inside of yourself that expend too much energy on what is missing or wrong. You create space for the good energy needed to appreciate all that is right.

Gratitude starts with a moment and evolves into a habit.

Today, I am grateful we have crossed paths in life and that you are willing to shift your perception and create your most connected life.

What are you grateful for right now? Think it, say it, write it down, own it.

There is nothing of value except that which resonates with you. Stop giving away energy to that which does not resonate.

Most people expend energy on other people, environments, technology, and thoughts that do not resonate, instead of people, environments, technology, and thoughts that do.

Can you imagine the quality of your life if you could do the reverse? You could have so much more peace.

THE PEACE AND WAR OF THE FIVE VOICES

There are five voices influencing the quality of your life.

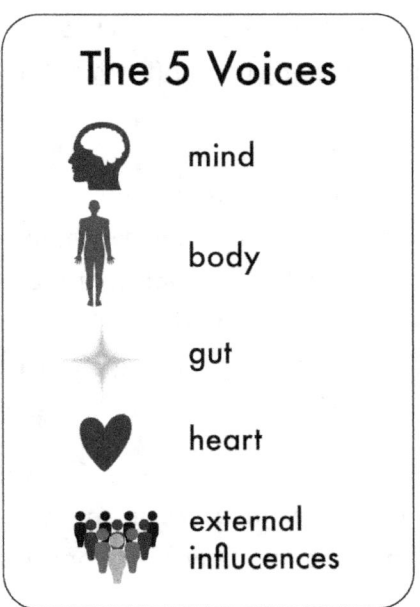

1. The Mind

This is where the ego lives. The ego is dominant, a bit of a know-it-all, and otherwise known as the boss or head honcho.

2. The Body

This voice is an incredible alarm with a built-in notification system, constantly alerting you with critical information like physical pain or feelings of stress or discomfort.

3. The Gut

This is your spirit voice, your most trusted advisor. Remember, you came with this voice, and it is quite literally you.

4. The Heart

The heart is beautiful, with good intentions, but it can be weak. For example, the heart has sentiments like *I guess I will loan them the money one more time or I love them so much, even though I am not treated well*. The heart is loving yet confusing at times.

5. All External Influences

This voice reflects the external influences from people, environments, and technology. It includes everyone and everything outside of yourself. Can you imagine the energy from the voices of external influences impacting you every year, month, week, day, hour, and second? It's a lot of chatter, which produces a lot of energy. You are going to need exceptional navigational skills to manage all this energy.

Sometimes, the voices collaborate, as if they have made an agreement with one another. They feel aligned, like one peaceful voice. Other times, they feel conflicted, as if they are at war with one another.

One voice affects all voices, much like the sounds of a symphony. The instruments contribute individually, but the cohesiveness creates the music. When the strings of a badly tuned violin are played, you experience a screeching jolt, alerting you that something is off. Pay attention to your jolts. They are the screeches in your symphony.

Your voices are unique, but it's their cohesiveness that allows them to function as a choir. You want them working together, the right way.

Your awareness helps you understand the individual voices, agendas, and unique communication styles of your five voices. The most beautiful music is produced from this awareness. The goal is to harmonize your voices so they are more aligned with a connected life. You create the harmony through your actions.

Make sure you are creating cohesive music. You are the conductor.

The most important voice, the gut, the spirit within you, is often the most neglected. The ego wants to convince you of its importance, and why wouldn't it, since it is usually the one in charge? It's time to let the ego know there is a shift in power and there is a new sheriff in town.

If you are feeling like you have lost touch with your inner voice, it's okay. Your inner voice does not judge you, and it will patiently wait for you to pick back up where you left off. Your inner voice is always working on your behalf.

When you connect with your inner voice, it is, in fact, a reunion. You already know each other. You have been here before.

Become aware of which voice is influencing you, what story it tells you, and the agenda it is following. Every voice has an agenda. The agenda of the gut voice is to educate you about awareness, authenticity, and self-trust and keep you on your most connected path.

Connecting with your five voices will strengthen your common sixth sense skills. How can you connect with these voices?

1. Listening

You must pause and pay attention. We are experts at mindlessly experiencing our days in highly productive (or unproductive) states, ignoring the alarms and responding only when we get knocked down so hard that we can barely get up.

Slow down. Listen. Pause. Pay Attention.

2. Having Awareness

The more you pay attention to your five voices, the more skilled you become at navigating them. Get curious about the flood of messages entering your sacred space. Ask yourself, "What voice is this message or jolt originating from?"

3. Reclaiming Your Power

You will notice a shift from receiver to navigator. Do you want to be at the mercy of all these voices, or do you want to be a proactive participant? Decide what messages to honor or dismiss. Ask, "What messages drain my energy? What messages energize me? Does this message resonate?"

This book (my voice) is an external voice entering and influencing your energy space. You decide what works for you. Embrace what resonates and filter out what does not. With common sixth sense, you have room for what serves you but limited space for what does not.

Use this same technique each time you get jolted. Reflect, analyze it, and get more curious. This curiosity will provide insightful knowledge.

Curiosity = Knowledge = Awareness = Self-Awareness

4. Taking Action

Awareness is great, but unless you act, there is no energy shift. Sometimes, doing nothing is the best course of action if you have made this decision consciously and purposefully.

5. Being Extra Cautious About Influence

Never be a passive consumer (or absorber) of energy from external influences. You are never at the mercy of people, environments, or technology (or your own thoughts) unless you believe you are.

Listen to the external voices and decide if you want to accept the message or not. That is your choice to make. Take an inquisitive approach when making your determination. For example, just because someone says that's the way you're supposed to do something doesn't mean it aligns with your mindset or the quality of life you seek. How will you possibly know unless you question it?

Your curiosity about the five voices will provide you with the knowledge and awareness needed to get closer to your most connected life.

It is a lot to navigate, but rest assured that you do not have to navigate all of this on your own.

TEAM SPIRIT

You have a spiritual support team working on your behalf every day. You are never alone. I know you have lonely times (I do too), but I promise that you are never alone. You have an incredible team on your side—always have and always will. Perhaps no one has ever taught you about your team or how to connect with them, but I will. Your team is remarkable because the players know you better than anyone. By working together, you gain more peace and trust in your life and get to enjoy the incredible benefits that come from teamwork.

Your team is one of the greatest resources in your life.

Remember, spirituality is your sacred connection to yourself, others, and whatever it is that you believe in that is bigger than yourself.

You build your team with your sacred connections. Follow these steps:

1. Assign Your Team

Think about what or who you connect with. Perhaps it is the ocean, the earth, God, or the Buddha. Think about loved ones (people and animals) who have passed away. Your team should consist of energies you feel a strong connection to. It's that simple.

Examples of teams:

- God, Jesus, angels, your grandpa, your friend, and your beloved dog.
- Angels, the earth, a parent or mentor who has passed, and the Buddha.

There are no rules when assigning your team. Don't limit the number of players—go big or scale down if you prefer. Some days, you may only want to connect with your grandpa; other days, you may have space for everyone. You can also substitute players in and out as needed.

2. Start Communicating with Your Team

Don't look up at the sky. We have been sold on the idea that our loved ones are floating around in the clouds. They are not. Look in front of you, behind you, next to you, and within you. This is the space they exist in. Remember, energy is everywhere.

Try connecting with your team in the morning when you wake up or when you are about to fall asleep. Running errands or exercising? Talk to your team.

3. Ask for What You Want

Confused about what to ask for? The answer is anything and everything. They are already supporting you and loving you. The more aware you become, the more you will understand and appreciate their support. You are never taking anything away from them (a question I get asked a lot). Ask for what you want, and they will bring you what you need.

Do you need support in parenting or building confidence in a new relationship? Are you seeking resources to manage chronic pain, grow your business, find job opportunities, navigate a difficult friendship, or simply gather the strength to get through the day? Talk to your team, just like you would talk to anyone. You can speak out loud or privately in your mind. Your team loves and supports you unconditionally. They are working hard on your behalf. It is time for you to be involved in the process of asking and receiving.

If you do not know what you want, just strike up a conversation with your team and see where it takes you.

4. Do Not Assign Expectations to Your Asks

Your team will always bring you what you need, so understand that it may or may not look like your expectation, but it will be orchestrated with the best intentions and outcome.

5. Acknowledge and Appreciate Resources When They Come

Your team has always been—and will always be—protecting and guiding you. Make sure you say, "Thank you" or "I understand why I needed that" when they deliver.

How do you know when they deliver? Oh, you will know. That is when your intuition takes center stage.

6. Never Stop

Just like any valued, quality relationship, your participation is key. This is two-way communication. You are not simply at the mercy of receiving, but you are, in fact, an active participant. Keep an open dialogue with your team daily. Nurture the relationship, make it a priority, and commit to strengthening the connections.

You may have been taught how to pray, which is a beautiful path to connection. Keep doing that if it resonates with you. Team communication and prayer are similar in that they are both deliberate, active communication. However, your communication with your team may ultimately become more casual and conversational than prayer. You will come to understand the difference over time as your relationships strengthen. You may also find that prayer and team connection sometimes overlap. Some people discover deep connection while participating in meditation. Do what works for you and then keep doing it.

Spirituality is a foundation for connection.

STAY IN YOUR VEHICLE

Your purpose in life is not to drive someone else's car. You can give them directions, help fix a tire, or give them a ride when they need to visit the repair shop, but do not drive their car.

People will give you directions whether you ask for them or not. Never hand over the keys to your vehicle and become the passenger. The safest and healthiest place for you is in the driver's seat of your own car.

Service your vehicle frequently, as this will reduce the chance of breakdowns.

There is nothing of value except that which resonates with you. Do not give time and energy to that which does not resonate.

Avoid people who waste your time and energy. If you cannot avoid them, manage your energy when you interact with them. Becoming aware of how much of your energy you mindlessly give away to them, even when you are not interacting with them, is critical to understanding your own energy management or mismanagement.

Are you depleting your own energy through exhaustive thoughts, physical manifestations in your body, or by repeatedly talking about them to others? Why?

SEE THE LIGHT

Imagine a flawless, majestic white light surrounding you, traveling through your body, engulfing you, and protecting you from any negative energy that tries to penetrate your space.

If you are ever at a complete loss as to how to protect your energy, try this visualization. (It's what I do when I am about to have a dreaded conversation or go to the DMV.)

THE RECIPE

Like any exceptional recipe, your recipe for a more connected and authentic life will take practice to perfect. There are so many factors that can influence our recipe results, such as time, temperature, directions, and amounts. We do our best, given the resources we have. Even after one shares their recipe, the recipient may experience better or worse results.

This is why: in attempting to use my recipe for connected living, you may have elements that work well and others that do not. The secret ingredient in the recipe for your most connected life can only be created and refined by you.

This creation and subsequent discovery will only occur through trial and error.

It's time to start putting your own spin on this recipe.

What ingredients do you have so far?

The Breath
Always breathe first.

Mindfulness
Stay present on purpose without judgment. Become aware of whatever you were not previously aware of.

Energy Management
Have an action plan in place for when you get jolted. Use the jolt-to-action technique.

A Wide Lens
Your life lens should be widening. If it is getting narrower, you are going in the wrong direction. Stop. Go back the other way!

An Air Filter

You, and only you, can filter negative energies from your life.

Awareness

Awareness gives you information. Use it.

Self-Awareness

Your awareness in life provides you with the space to self-reflect and examine your own behaviors, opinions, attitudes, and mindsets. This information becomes your self-awareness.

Spirituality

Your relationship with your spirit and that which is bigger than you should be nurtured, prioritized, and appreciated, just like any other relationship you value.

Faith

Your life has meaning. You have a purpose in this world. Your belief in whatever you believe in will lead you deeper into your exploration of self.

Start experimenting with the ingredients you have so far in your recipe.

You will start to see that the recipe will not work unless the ingredients work together to create a harmony of flavors. It is the synergy that creates the perfect comfort food. One ingredient cannot function properly without the others.

I remember my first 333 recipes. Each one carried me closer to my most authentic and connected life.

Never stop experimenting with your recipe.

DEATH TO EXPECTATIONS

Let your expectations die so you can be free. We have all designated ourselves the directors of life. We have created expectations for the people around us (the cast), the environment (the set designs), our bodies (wardrobe, hair, and makeup), and ourselves (the lead actor, of course).

There are multiple production phases in the creation of a movie. No epic movie was made without excellent editing. In many productions, actors ad lib to create the most memorable scenes. If you let your expectations die, you save energy to be more free-spirited (ad lib) and adjust (edit) your life as it unfolds. Forget imagining a perfect production, where everything falls into place when you sternly demand, "Action!" It's a dream, not a reality, and you suffer because of it.

You should still dream—dream big, be ambitious, and have high standards—but not at your own demise. Do you see the difference? If you frequently suffer from disappointment and try to control outcomes, examine the expectations of the production you have created. Don't ever stop being the director of your own life, but accept that the beginning, middle, and end may not follow the script. Letting go of expectations helps quiet perfectionism and your need for control. It can lessen your anxiety so you can genuinely enjoy the epic movie that is your life. The people around you will appreciate it, and the popcorn will taste even better.

Tap into your soul's voice. This voice says all people and environments are filled with imperfections because we were designed this way so we could evolve and grow. By accepting this truth and surrendering the fantasy of expectations, you have plenty of room to stay present and focus on what is versus what is not.

Consider removing expectations and adding more natural, organic ingredients to your recipe.

Who you are = your spirit

What you have = your blessings

What you don't have = what you think you need

What you want = your goals and aspirations

What you need = your soul's truth

What you want and what you need are not the same thing. Your spirit knows *exactly* what you need.

You have learned—and continue to learn throughout this book—that reconnecting with your spirit, thereby gaining more self-trust and personal power, enables you to live a more authentic life. This life is rightfully yours. Think about the behavior of a rebellious teen at the mercy of their environment, seeking attention and control as they attempt to navigate feelings and circumstances. As an adult, you are no longer at the mercy of your influences. There is no need for rebellion, only connection. Self-connection, tools, and a management system will help you navigate your life circumstances better. Remember, the goal is to thrive, not simply survive. Surviving will get you through it, and I have no doubt you have served your time in survival mode, but you do not have to spend the rest of your extraordinary life simply surviving. I have done both, and thriving is so much better.

ORBITS

There is nothing quite like gazing at the sky on a crystal-clear night. It is mind-blowing to consider the vastness of our solar system and beyond. There are opposing perspectives on the energies that glitter in our night skies—from the Babylonians' creation of the zodiac to Greek philosophers contemplating the power of the sun to modern-day scientists exploring the significance of newly discovered exoplanets. Regardless of these differing views, we cannot deny the powerful influence that exists around us.

What energies are orbiting around you? What people? What environments? What thoughts? What stories?

How much power do you give them? How often do you allow them to throw you off-balance? When a person, environment, technology, or even your own thoughts are out of balance, you will be, too—unless you have an energy management system in place. When you are off-balance, the people and environments you orbit will be, too—unless they have an energy management system in place.

There is an entire world of people who exist beyond the way you are existing. There is nothing wrong with the way you currently exist in this world—unless you do not want to exist this way.

There is a world that offers greater energy freedom, deeper connection, and more authenticity—a world you were meant to live and thrive in—and it is rightfully yours to claim. Are you claiming it?

How do you access this world? There must be an energy shift. There are opportunities every single day for you to make a shift. You cannot make a shift without taking ownership of your energy management.

CHAPTER SIX

THE FREEDOM

Imagine the freedom that comes from ownership. If I take responsibility, the ownership is mine.

Responsibility often carries negative connotations, as we associate it with stress and work overload, treating it as the scapegoat that robs us of leisure time. People say, "I do not want the responsibility" or "I have too much responsibility."

On the flip side, responsibility can be extremely positive. Responsibility is about having more influence over outcomes. Have you noticed that people who take responsibility are more reliable and likely to meet their goals? I am not going to hire someone irresponsible to care for my dogs when I travel. We value responsible people and lean into those who will come through for us, but when it comes to the absolute ownership of our own quality of life, sometimes we fall short and avoid responsibility at all costs. And it certainly costs us when we do.

Why would you ever give the responsibility for your quality of life to someone else?

Responsibility is a gift. Unwrap it. Never, ever regift it.

Now that you have unwrapped and accepted the gift of responsibility, move forward with full commitment.

Commit to better self-care. Self-care is not selfish. Whoever or whatever gave you that impression misled you. Your mind, body, and spirit need your care. You must become a reliable caretaker for the person you love—you. When you decide to take better care of yourself and commit to focusing your energy on what serves your greater well-being, you will simultaneously experience the undoing of that which no longer serves you. Each time you take action based on a conscious, purposeful choice that serves your well-being, you are reducing suffering.

We associate self-care with exercise, free time, or getting enough sleep. Yes, those are valuable and necessary ways to take care of yourself, but what about the self-care needed when you get a jolt?

Take conscious, purposeful action when you get jolted. A jolt is an alarm, a notification alerting you that something does not vibe.

Consider a jolt an opportunity to reduce suffering. Negative jolts hurt our spirit. They are the messengers of a disconnect.

Addressing a jolt in real time is the absolute best form of self-care because it will decrease present-moment suffering. As a bonus, it will decrease the potential future suffering that prevents you from living your most authentic and connected life.

Jolt + Reaction = Disconnection

Jolt + Purposeful Action = Connection

What you do with awareness, you undo in suffering.

Examples:

- Doing: Limiting conversation with energy vampires
- Undoing: The tension you feel in your shoulders when you spend long periods of time getting the life sucked out of you
- Undoing: Resentment
- Doing: Deciding to alter your diet and not going for long periods of time without eating

- Undoing: The jolt of a blood sugar dip or having a hangry reaction toward another person
- Undoing: Ignoring your body's voice when it tells you it needs more balance
- Doing: Shifting your perspective of your work environment by consciously choosing to make today better than yesterday
- Undoing: Repeating a story about the belief that you do not have any power to make your work experience better
- Undoing: Dependency on an external environment to determine your quality of life

You benefit tremendously from practicing self-care for your mind, body, and spirit. Every person and environment you encounter benefits from your self-care and ability to manage jolts.

The goal is a connected *lifestyle*.

Practice self-care every single day.

Just the act of staying more present improves self-care. Consciously keep your mind on the business that is right in front of you and take notice of what you did not notice before.

Self-connection = more consistent self-care

Think about someone you love and feel close to. To take the absolute best possible care of this person, you need to provide them with consistent love, time, energy, and support. You would not provide care, love, time, energy, and support to this person if you did not value and love them. They can certainly find value in the relationship as well, and they benefit greatly from it and the connection it provides.

Why would you provide all this energy to a person you do not value?

You are valuable. You deserve care, love, time, energy, and support, too.

Awareness = Purposeful Action

Awareness is one thing, but action is everything. Awareness is the catalyst for change. You change by taking action. Remember, sometimes doing nothing is the right action for you. The catalyst causes the reaction. Your action is your response to the catalyst.

The deeper your connection with yourself and the more care, love, time, energy, and support you give yourself, the greater the value and benefit and, most importantly, the stronger the connection.

Continue to explore the benefits of fitness, nutrition, and sleep; they are imperative for a connected life. But today, right now, incorporate more self-care by managing your jolts.

A jolt alerts you to prioritize your self-care.

Add self-care to your ingredient list.

Your recipe for a more connected life is coming together, and it is sounding so delicious.

SYSTEM OVERLOAD

Everything is a system. Is it inherently good or bad, or is it our management—or mismanagement—that determines how we experience it? A system is simply a system. Your management of that system determines the experience you assign to it.

How much energy do you waste away on the systems you participate in? Every system you participate in is attempting to create an algorithm for you. The systems proclaim they are working on your behalf, but how can they accurately determine this when you are the only person who can see clearly through your lens?

Everything is a system—home, education, technology, workplace, family, government, healthcare, etc.

You must be smarter than the systems, or they will annihilate your energy.

In my mindfulness-based self-development business, I work with many clients who feel powerless or at the mercy of their systems—until they realize they are not.

To be smarter than the systems, you must see yourself as separate from them. This can be challenging because some systems have good intentions, but that does not mean you have to adhere to those systems. Your parents, teachers, bosses, or doctors have good intentions, but remember, they only know their own lens of life. This is why it is imperative that you are your most trusted advisor. Only then will you understand if the systems' intentions are right for you.

This acknowledgment takes back your power. You decide what resonates through reflection and self-awareness and by leaning into your gut voice.

Just because someone says so does not make it so. You are never at the mercy of a system unless you surrender to it. Please do not do that.

Self-reflect for a moment. What systems are getting the best of you? What systems bring out the best in you?

Accept that everything you have exposure to is a system. That does not mean it is a bad system, but it does not mean it is a good system either. It is simply a system.

You determine how to healthily navigate the system. The system cannot healthily navigate life for you because it is a system and does not understand how to do that for you specifically. A system is made of parts that operate together to accomplish a goal. Systems are not designed for the individual.

Are you wasting precious energy on systems that are totally incapable of delivering what you need? We have all been there before.

The salmon swim upstream, exerting so much energy as they migrate back to their birthplace to reproduce. During this journey, some ultimately end up in the mouths of hungry grizzly bears. The bears are aware that the salmon are on a mission home from June to September each year. That is the way the system works. Sounds risky for the salmon, so why risk it? Because the salmon innately knows it must return home, and like any journey we take, there are risks.

Should you be like the salmon as you continue to journey back home to yourself, even with all the potential risks? Of course! The most connected space you can reside in is your home. You must get home.

Go on this journey with awareness and energy management so you can make it home alive.

It's the salmon's lack of awareness that is the death sentence, not necessarily the system itself.

You want to have the energy capacity to show up in the world. Don't waste it swimming upstream, just to end up in a bear's mouth.

The system is the system. The salmon must get home.

You must get home, too, and it will take effort and energy, but it does not have to be a futile effort.

Imagine you are the salmon. Now, try going around the bear or let another salmon get eaten instead. Sorry, not sorry. The doomed salmon should have had better energy management skills.

If you have allowed the systems in your life to steal your power, you did the best you could with what you knew at the time, but now you can do better.

Whatever you are involved in—work, school, home, relationships, etc.— understand that they are systems, and those systems are not specifically designed for you. You must learn how to navigate the systems so you suffer less. Be smart! Ask yourself these questions:

1. How does this system affect my energy?
2. How does this system affect my mind?
3. How does this system affect my body?
4. How does this system affect my spirit?
5. How can I be smarter than this system?

Stop mindlessly accepting energy and influence into your life and start mindfully navigating energy.

How do you become more mindful?

EVERYTHING AND NOTHING

There are many resources for mindful connection.

- Doing yoga
- Practicing meditation
- Journaling
- Making eye contact
- Breathing
- Expressing gratitude
- Protecting your energy
- Growing your mindset
- Connecting with your spiritual support team
- Paying attention to jolts
- Determining the point of origin from the five voices
- Listening to music
- Slowing down while eating
- Watching the sunset
- Telling someone you love them
- Noticing the texture of a tree
- Going toward what naturally pulls you in
- Listening
- Observing
- Hugging a loved one
- Pausing
- Increasing awareness during everyday tasks
- Feeling the sun on your face
- Performing acts of kindness without expectation

- Laughing
- Exploring the arts
- Spending time with animals
- Striking up a conversation with a stranger

One of the best ways to be mindful? Doing nothing but doing it consciously.

The most mindfully connected clients I have worked with were the ones who not only understood connection as a lifestyle but also accepted the responsibility of creating it.

They prioritize self-care. They are aware. They are reflective. They have an energy management system in place. They thrive. They consistently and actively participate. They understand that doing nothing is sometimes the best form of connection.

THE STORY ARC OF THE SOUL

Nothing is personal. It really isn't.

We are all here, participating in the systems, attempting to navigate the complexities of our minds, bodies, and spirits. Some people are good at it; others, not so much.

Every person comes with a story that is deeply embedded in their soul and incomprehensible to others. It is impossible for us to fully understand someone else's story. Of course, we can relate and show empathy, and we have commonalities, but only you can see clearly through your lens.

The more aware and connected you are, the better you recognize and appreciate the complexity of the human spirit, and the better you can give grace to others.

This does not mean we excuse bad behavior or allow anyone to treat us poorly.

We all have an inciting incident, a story arc, and, unfortunately, for some, a villain origin story. Believing you have all the insider information on a person's life is a fantasy. This should not be discouraging but empowering. Accepting that you cannot possibly know the complexity of the ins and outs of what makes a person who they are is freeing. Now, you can stop wasting so much energy on it.

So much of our suffering comes from how we mismanage other people's energy. If you consider the energy of a person and how you manage it (take purposeful action) or mismanage it (internalize, explode in anger, or ruminate), you'll see it is simply their energy—and how you respond to that energy is your *decision*.

I often ask people what they need to experience a more connected life.

Typically, people say they need:

- To participate in activities that bring me joy and fulfillment.
- To surround myself with people I enjoy being around.
- To stop juggling a million things and feeling overworked.
- To develop better time management skills.
- To have more silence.
- To have more free time.
- To improve my stress management.
- To find a different job.
- To be in a new relationship.
- To have more money.
- To feel appreciated.

I rarely hear people say they need:

- To deepen my self-connection.
- To explore my spirituality.
- To cultivate greater awareness.
- To practice more mindfulness.
- To strengthen my faith.
- To build a stronger relationship with myself.
- To develop energy management skills.

This represents the connection crisis.

HAVE MORE DISCERNING TASTE

My twelve-year-old dog, Mac—lovingly named after a Mack truck because he was found at a truck stop with eight broken bones—needed a Fleetwood. I have always loved the band Fleetwood Mac, and the song "Dreams" remains one of my favorites. For several years, I kept my eyes open and on the lookout for another dog already named Fleetwood, although he only existed in my imagination. I explored shelters on occasion, but to my dismay, I always left empty-handed, without my Fleetwood. Then I got the call. My husband was driving on a desolate highway during an ice storm in the south of Texas, and there he was, the divinely planted Fleetwood—a beautiful, fluffy, white Great Pyrenees and Dogue de Bordeaux mix (according to the DNA test). You may have a difficult time visualizing Fleetwood because he is so unique, confirmed by the excessive number of times I get stopped and asked, "What breed is he?"

My band is now complete, with my Fleetwood and my Mac, and they could not be more different. Mac, fittingly enough, is a truck stop kind of guy, motivated by food and playing catch. Fleetwood, on the other hand, is a bit more refined, stoic, and perfectly happy sitting in the sun and gazing at birds.

There is a bustling area near my home in Florida filled with restaurants and coffee shops, with art festivals on the weekends. Fleetwood loves a good stroll around this area, and while walking one day, I was approached by a production company and asked if Fleetwood would like to be in a feature highlighting a local business that makes ice pops. (Pardon me— they are locally sourced, made by hand, and not conventional ice cream but artisan ice pops.) A couple of their products are dog friendly, and Fleetwood was to be filmed consuming the watermelon ice pop.

And action!

After a couple of curious licks, Fleetwood was not having it. The host played it off by suggesting Fleetwood was indecisive, but I chimed in, stating, "Actually, he has very discerning taste."

Although that was the end of Fleetwood's acting career, and I was no longer a stage mom, I was reminded that authenticity is excellent.

Fleetwood could not have cared less about the expectation that he should have enjoyed the ice pop (artisan, locally sourced). Fleetwood was just being his quirky, authentic, highly refined self.

Be you more. Be discerning.

You cannot move forward unless you have an open mind and an open heart. I know you have both (or you would not be reading this book).

Keep moving forward.

TOTAL CHAOS

We experience chaos but are more equipped for calm. Thankfully, we have a built-in response system for extreme chaos—called the fight-or-flight response—where adrenaline and hormones surge through the body, prompting us to make life-or-death decisions to flee or fight.

If you are experiencing prolonged chaos and are chronically stressed, you know what an excruciating toll this state of being takes on your mind, body, and spirit. There are not enough pages in this book to cover the negative effects of stress, and you have probably heard most of it already.

Your fight-or-flight response means you are equipped for chaos. The resource is built-in and gets used with or without your consent because it is an automatic response.

But you are more equipped for calm. These resources are also built-in; you just may not know how to use them properly.

What resources can you use right now to soften the voices of your chaos and stress? Possibilities include:

- Faith
- Spirituality
- Mindfulness
- Energy management
- The breath
- The jolt-to-action technique
- The air purifier technique

Our lives are chaotic, complex, and overwhelming at times. Use what you innately possess to manage chaos, complexity, and overwhelm. Be proactive.

The breath, the jolt-to-action technique, and the air purifier technique are not going to eliminate chaos; however, they can certainly reduce suffering and get you closer to home, back to you, exactly where you belong.

But first, you must believe you deserve to go home.

I, _____, give myself permission to live my most connected and authentic life.

_____

Signature and Date

Consider the level of chaos you are experiencing.

What are the levels?

Level 1 = General annoyances and everyday disruptions

Level 2–9 = Everything in between

Level 10 = Fight or flight

Don't give away so much energy to level 1 experiences, or to levels 2, 3, or 4, for that matter. It is simply not worth the energy effort, considering the negative effects of stress.

Making the decision not to give energy away is a purposeful action. If you choose not to make this decision, it is a mindless reaction that adds stress and chaos to your life. Before you make the decision, you need to have the awareness that you are giving energy away in the first place.

How can you have more awareness? By being more mindful.

RISK = REWARD

So many people I speak with are not living authentically. They feel authenticity causes obstacles or is unattainable. They depend on others to clear the obstacles out of their paths, desperately leaning on others for answers.

What they fail to understand is that there are no obstacles. You are already authentic.

Everyone benefits from your authenticity. People gravitate toward authenticity.

I have seen this repeatedly in education when working with criminal justice graduate students. Many are ill-prepared for the much-dreaded public speaking required for their capstone research (which is similar to a thesis but is only one semester instead of a full year). Ironically, in class, we focus less on the presentation skills and more on mindfulness, authenticity, and connection, which ultimately produces better speakers. They all perform best when they extract and incorporate the authentic self into the final, faculty-judged presentation.

What is authenticity? Being true to yourself. When was the last time you did that?

You are already authentic. You came like this.

Are you being true to yourself?

The contents of this book are not about changing you; they are about changing the way you manage energy and extracting your innate resources. You are still authentically you, whether you read this book or not.

I have seen consistent behaviors in people who struggle to express authenticity.

1. **We are self-conscious.** This is the mind (ego) voice dominating. I hate when it does that.

2. **We don't understand our own authenticity.** The more connected you are to yourself, the closer you become to your authentic self. As long as you are willing to gain more clarity, you will. It is a magical thing that happens when our spiritual support team cranks up the volume for us when we are finally willing to listen.

Awareness = Self-Connection

It is okay if you do not understand your authenticity right now because you have awareness, and that is all the guidance you need to start the journey.

You must take risks if you want to unleash your authenticity. Yes, even if you might be judged. People are doing that anyway, so what's the difference?

Sometimes, the best way to be more authentic is to say f*** it and take the risk—go for it.

UNLEASH THE FREE SPIRIT

Imagine you are a house. Your spirit is experiencing life inside your house. Your house is literally you. That must be such a unique and fascinating place for it to exist.

What is it like inside of you? Does it resemble a house you frantically try to keep perfect while preparing for visitors or in the event someone unexpectedly stops by? Is it a fraternity house? I'll spare you that description. Is it your authentic house?

Your spirit wants to live comfortably in your house, but you must put out the welcome mat, open the door, and let it in.

Be mindful of the house you share with your spirit. The perfect house for you is beautiful, authentic, and most importantly, a comfortable space for you to live your most connected life.

If you do not feel like your house is comfortable right now, do not worry; your spirit will help you go house hunting for your perfect home. You won't have to look far to find it.

Your spirit chose your house. Your spirit chose you.

You are beautiful and authentic, and you deserve to experience a comfortable, connected life.

Your spirit wants to be unleashed. Is your spirit leashed up inside of you like a guard dog (overly protective, standing on its hind legs, with exposed teeth) or more like a leashed puppy (curious, playful, and blindly loving to all)? Either way, your spirit is on a leash, and your life story, experiences, perception, and lens put it there. That is not good or bad; it just is.

It is not healthy to be on a leash for too long. Psychological stress, lack of socialization, safety concerns, mobility issues, and discomfort are results of being leashed for prolonged periods of time.

If you keep holding back your authenticity, you can expect more suffering.

Each time you honor your authenticity, you loosen the leash.

What would it feel like to remove the leash?

THE STORYTELLER

Every story we tell about someone else is not their story. It is the story we have concocted based on our interpretation of their story.

People can drive us nuts! Venting about them can be cathartic, but it should have a beginning and an end and not be ongoing. If it does not have an ending, you have most likely designated yourself as the storyteller of another person's life, behaviors, or perspectives. If you are still getting equally worked up in response to the behaviors of another person as you did days, weeks, or years ago, you are not managing your energy properly. You are still suffering in the storyline.

Be mindful of negative storytelling. Most stories about other people tend to be pessimistic or cynical and are not particularly compelling, especially because they tend to get repeated. It is an energy drain for the recipient, and most people cannot wait for these stories to conclude.

The negative stories we tell about ourselves are even more painful to listen to, causing us to suffer on repeat. You must get so sick of hearing these stories.

You can change a story at any time if you have awareness and energy management skills. Become aware of your stories and start writing new ones.

An authentic storyteller can create a bestseller.

Pro tip: Be especially aware if you classify yourself as a "good" listener. This is an honorable skill to have and is necessary for a connected life, but without boundaries, you can easily attract people who are not capable of reciprocating and who will blatantly abuse your time and ability to show up for others.

Having awareness and connecting with yourself can not only help you better navigate daily life stressors but can also evolve into profound life shifts. Awareness not only benefits you, but it also benefits every person and every environment you encounter.

Reminder: Awareness is the result of mindfulness, simply noticing something you have not previously noticed.

Your awareness can create profound shifts, changing the trajectory of negative experiences, such as parenting styles and inherited trauma. You have the power to spare the next generation from suffering and potentially impact the previous generation. Remember, you can inspire others with your wide lens and your connected actions.

Did you have a parent who emotionally neglected you, was dismissive or overprotective, placed too many responsibilities on you, or exposed you to family conflict?

You do not have to be that parent. You can break the cycle. However, you cannot break the cycle if you are not aware. When you have awareness, assume responsibility for energy management, and take purposeful action, you can break the cycle.

Your behavior, self-care, and energy management will be noted by others. This will have a profoundly positive impact on the next generation.

Think of something your parent or caretaker did that affected you negatively. Think of something you do that may affect your children or the people closest to you negatively. Are there parallels?

Examples:

- Are you critical? Was a parent critical?
- Do you retreat during difficult conversations? Did a parent retreat during difficult conversations?

- Are you a complainer? Was your caretaker a complainer?

These behaviors have a tremendous energy influence on the people who surround you. They most certainly had an energy impact on you, right?

Become aware. Make a small energy shift. Your energy will be noted. Your energy will be different. Everyone will benefit.

But first, you must want to make a change. Do you?

Reminder: You cannot change others, but you can inspire them with your own actions.

Awareness is nothing without action.

Awareness is a mixed blessing. It provides so much valuable information as we explore ourselves, others, and the world, but it needs to be used properly. Yes, you must also have an awareness about your awareness.

Be cautious of hyperawareness. This can contribute to anxiety. If you are finding yourself hypervigilant about everyone and everything, this is not healthy awareness.

Be cautious about perfectionism; it might look impressive from the outside, but it exists chaotically inside of you.

You must give yourself permission to be human, to explore, and to find the awareness balance best suited to you.

Awareness is meant to enhance your life. If you feel like you are experiencing awareness overload, noticing everything and everyone, take a break and regroup.

We are all human, which means we can be empathic or apathetic, compassionate or indifferent, calm or a hot mess of chaos. It is what it is. We are human. You must allow yourself grace. Use the information obtained from your less desirable moments and grow from them. We are all ill-behaved sometimes. It's called being human.

No person is connected and authentic all the time. This is so far out of reach that it is impossible and an unhealthy expectation.

People think or say, "You wouldn't understand; it's complicated."

Life is complicated by design; otherwise, how can we discover balance, free will, transformation, or connection?

It is our job to make our lives less complicated.

USE YOUR GOD-GIVEN TALENTS

At some point, most of us reflect on life and realize *If I only knew then what I know now. If I had leaned into myself more—trusted my intuition and addressed my needs—life would have been, well… different. I should have used my natural resources more.*

What are your natural resources? What is your God-given (or whatever you believe in) talent? Is it your kindness, intellect, singing voice, business acumen, athletics, or dance ability?

Now, think beyond these talents and think about other types of gifts, like intuition, gut instinct, or the breath. Do you keep these buried away in the bottom of your toolbox?

Where the hell did I put those?

You do not have to dig through a bottomless pit to locate them. They are accessible, always.

Make your tools more readily available and use them. Work with what you already have and what you are developing.

- Breath
- Awareness
- Energy
- Gratitude
- Intuition
- Gut Instinct

REGRETS

Past regrets do not serve you now, but awareness and knowledge do.

Now you know. Now you are more aware.

I should have trusted my gut. I did not realize how good I had it. I should have taken better care of myself. Yada yada yada.

This is life.

Regrets do not serve you in the present moment.

We hear the well-intended advice or last words of the elderly as they reflect on their lives.

- Don't chase perfection.
- Live without fear.
- Enjoy life.
- Be kind.
- Value relationships.

While there is much appreciation for the advice, most people opt to ignore it, choosing to go about their regular business and attempting to figure it all out on their own.

We are still going to chase perfection, live with fear, not enjoy life, and not be kind sometimes. The key is to manage the jolts of fear, perfectionism, sadness, or disrespect when they present themselves.

You cannot manage anything that you are not aware of. A jolt will make you aware. The breath will decrease the jolt. Intercept the energy jolts and manage them before they become regrettable reflections you make at ninety years old.

Awareness is nothing without action.

How do we become more aware? Be more . . .?
Hint: It starts with an *m*.

Mindfulness = Awareness = Self-Awareness

DO YOUR BEST AND FORGET THE REST

Okay, that seems simple enough—except for the part where most people never actually forget the rest.

If you aren't mindfully aware, how can you truly do your best—purposefully and intentionally—in support of your most authentic, connected life?

You are exerting a lot of energy just trying to do your best, and you are exerting even more trying to forget the rest.

Let's work smarter, not harder.

Imagine a life where you can do your best with purposeful action.

Remember, you are working toward shifting from surviving to thriving. There are, of course, significant times in our lives when we need to be in survival mode and do our best to just get through each day, and that is more than enough. For all the other days, try to be mindful and gain information to maximize your energy output so you can continue to shift from surviving to thriving.

THE HIDDEN GEM

Let's go on a treasure hunt. Do whatever it takes to find the treasure chest, for it will be filled with gold coins, gems, jewels, and treasure maps.

Along the way, you will encounter hostile terrain, treacherous weather, deceit, curses, and possibly mutiny.

Finally, the treasure chest! Inside, the treasure map. Where will it lead you? Is it an accurate map, or are you headed straight into an ambush?

Why are we always on a treacherous quest for answers from someone else or somewhere else, often relying on inaccurate maps along the way?

Why are we trying to interpret a map someone else created based on their interpretation of how we should be, where we should go, and what we should think?

Try following your own intuitive guidance and skip the scurvy.

Open your innate treasure chest. You already have the map inside. The map is your soul's voice, and it will lead you exactly where you need to go.

CHAPTER SEVEN

THE BLUE LINE

On a trip to Marrakesh, I became mesmerized by the cobalt blues spread throughout this ancient and enchanting city. Even when intermixed with the vibrant colors of saffron and turmeric spread throughout the souks, my spirit still gravitated to the Majorelle, indigo, and cobalt blues. Blue represents tranquility, spirituality, peacefulness, and calm, like settled-down, end-of-day ocean tides.

When you get jolted, you must make a decision. Remember, reaction is disconnection. If you take purposeful, conscious action, you are connected. You cannot act unless you have made the decision to do so.

You need a tool to make the best decision.

The Blue Line

Decision-Making Tool

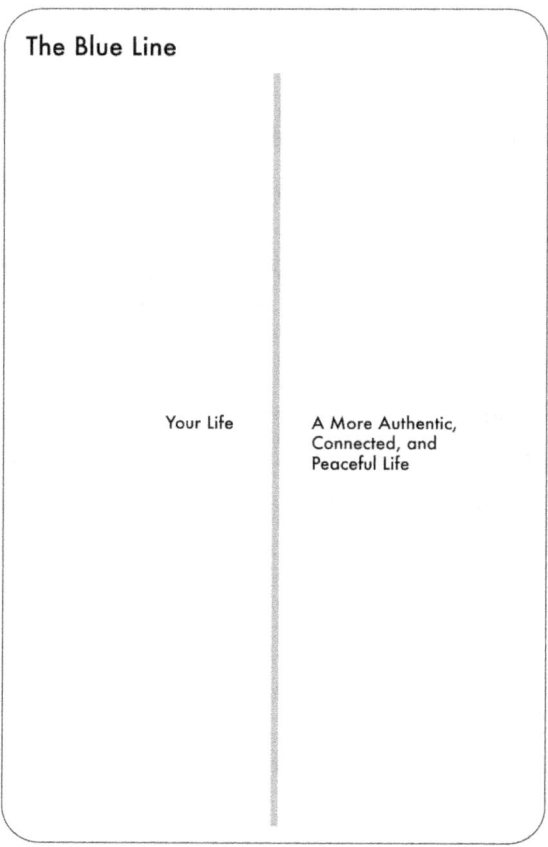

Due to the black-and-white print of this book, you must imagine a blue line.

What shade of blue is your line? Is it azure, sapphire, or sky blue?

Imagine your blue line in your mind. Imagine your blue line in your heart. Imagine your blue line in your spirit.

The blue line is going to help you make more authentic and connected decisions.

How do you make the best decisions to get you closer to a more connected life? You use the blue line.

The blue line represents your two lives. The left side represents the life you live now, and the right side represents your more authentic, connected life. One side of the line is what you know now (your lens of life), and on the other is how you grow and expand your lens.

How do you cross the blue line? You make a connected, conscious decision after you receive a jolt.

Every time you get a jolt, try to use the blue line.

Imagine the blue line in your mind, keep it close to your heart, or tattoo it on your hand. Do whatever it takes to keep it accessible.

When you are sitting in traffic, imagine the blue line. When you spend time with low-vibration people, imagine the blue line. When you feel overwhelmed, imagine the blue line. When the server messes up your order, imagine the blue line. When you are doomscrolling, imagine the blue line. When your sibling upstages you once again, imagine the blue line. When people do not agree with you, imagine the blue line. When you hold back from sharing your voice, imagine the blue line.

The blue line is not about other people, environments, or technology. It is about you and only you.

Ask yourself, "What side of the blue line am I on right now? Then ask, "What side of the blue line do I want to be on?" Most importantly, ask yourself, "What conscious decision do I want to make in this jolted moment to get to the right side of the blue line, where my most authentic and connected life awaits?"

There is deeper connection and more peace on the right side.

People say, "Don't cross the line." Please, by any means, cross the blue line. This is the one line you absolutely want to cross.

This does not mean you change who you are; this means you decide you will honor your most connected self, and you will disengage from that which makes you feel disconnected and no longer serves you.

This line will deceptively feel like a finish line. It is not. It is a starting line.

You have experienced so much in your life and worked tremendously hard to navigate it, and for that, you should be commended. But what if you can do consistently better? What if you can work smarter, not harder?

The blue line will help you manage negative energy better so you can suffer less. Regardless of where you are now or what you have experienced in your life, you deserve to suffer less. Energy management reduces suffering. You reduce suffering every time you cross the blue line.

The blue line is always the starting line that propels you toward your most connected life. Think of a runner awaiting the sound of the starting pistol, pushing against the starting block, ready to accelerate. The blue line helps you accelerate your life forward.

Remember, it is your action that gets you to the right side of the blue line.

It is time to start leaving behind the negative energy; it's draining your spirit. How drained is your spirit? Are you honoring your spirit?

Lean into the blue line as guidance for your best decision-making. You are your best guide after all.

The decision to cross the blue line comes from your soul's voice. Your soul's voice knows what you need. It makes you blatantly aware when energy is draining and depleting you or inspiring and motivating you.

Your life will have more depth and energy freedom on the right side of the line. That is why it is called the *right* side.

Why would you ever give up your freedom?

THE HERO AND THE VILLAIN

When you take bold steps toward honoring the needs of your body, mind, and spirit, you can inspire others through your actions. However, not everyone is going to be excited or encouraged by your energy shifts.

Shifting your energy toward your most connected life is a gift to yourself.

Some people will want to return the gift ("Hey, did this come with a gift receipt?") or penalize, even villainize, you for your newfound shifts and energy boundary setting.

Remind yourself that those who respond this way do not have a healthy energy management system of their own, so how can they possibly understand yours?

Most people's responses will fall somewhere in between being inspired and maligning.

Understand that as we shift, we must be both the hero and the villain. Be the hero for yourself and be okay with the fact that others may not resonate with your awareness because they no longer benefit from your lack of it.

If you cannot accept this truth, you will continue to mindlessly give your energy freedom away to the people and environments you desire to conserve it from in the first place. Make that make sense.

How do you know if you are on the wrong side of the blue line?

Are you reacting to jolts? Forgetting to use your breath? Is your level of suffering staying the same? Are you internalizing? Are you lashing out at others?

The jolts are not the enemy; they are the opportunity. They remind us of our unfinished energy business. You can run, but you cannot hide. Our unfinished business loves to creep up on us to remind us that we still have work to do, surprising us sometimes years later. "Boo!" Like a horror movie jump scare.

I know, I wish my unfinished business would leave me alone, too.

Think of how much wider your intuitive lens will get when you apply the blue line decision-making tool.

I can already see it expanding.

Remember, the expansion occurs from purposeful action, not just awareness.

Can you feel your intuitive lens getting bigger, widening, evolving, and resulting in expanded perceptions of self and others?

Let's recap:

1. Jolt.
2. Breath.
3. Get back in your body. Get the jolts of energy out!
4. Act. Use the blue line to make more connected decisions.

Some energy jolts can quickly detach (for example, when the barista forgets to put the agave in your iced green tea). Some energy jolts take a little more time to fully exit (for example, when a friend's comment really stings). Other jolts can take years to dissipate from your mind, body, and spirit (for example, when you finally release the anger and sadness from the betrayal or abuse that has crept up on you repeatedly throughout your life). Getting to say goodbye to those jolts is the best feeling of all.

If you are using your awareness to take purposeful action that supports your best quality of life, you are strengthening your relationship with yourself and decreasing your suffering.

SACRED ENERGY

Whomever you share your energy with will receive your energy—the positive energy, the negative energy, and the neutral energy. Wherever you put your attention, time, or focus will receive your attention, time, or focus, otherwise known as your energy.

Every person who gets your attention also gets your energy—positive, negative, or neutral. The people in your immediate circle (friends, family, and coworkers) own a piece of your energy, and you own a piece of their energy as well. The people and environments you cross paths with every day receive your energy, too.

Energy is emitted, and energy is absorbed.

What kind of energy are you sharing with the world? How much of your energy are people and environments extracting from you with or without your permission? How much of their energy are you absorbing?

Everything you own owns a piece of you because everything is energy. How much of others' energy do you want to own?

Think about the people in your life. Which of these people occupies the most space and time in your mind, your heart, and your soul? Consider both the positive and negative people.

Do you occupy that kind of space in their lives? Hmmm . . . something to think about.

Be very cognizant about who occupies energy space within you. If someone is staying in your house, they are using your water, your electricity, and your energy. Never let anyone live rent-free or be a squatter in your mind, body, or spirit. If they get to stay, it is because you have decided that the energy you exert on them elevates your life.

I am not suggesting you start cutting people out of your life simply because they don't elevate your life. I am suggesting that you are responsible for approving their rent application and allowing them to be tenants. You must be a conscious property manager of energy. You have the right to evict.

Awareness = Self-Awareness = Less Suffering

You alone control the amount of space someone can occupy within you.

Let's do a quick test.

Think of two people who both require your energy. One person produces positive energy, and the other produces negative energy. How do you feel around these people? Take note of the sensations in your body. The energy in your body tells you everything you need to know.

The coolest thing about awareness is that once you have it, you cannot not have it.

It continuously expands.

I want to lessen your struggle by providing resources to help you navigate life better.

You are doing an incredible job so far. Shifting your mindset and incorporating new ideas is challenging. It requires vulnerability, commitment, emotional maturity, and a sense of adventure.

It can be a real struggle sometimes. And here you are, doing it.

If you feel like you need extra support, you most likely do. Reach out to a friend, family member, doctor, or therapist. There are always additional resources available to you. The first step, for some, can be the hardest part. When you take the first step, you cross the blue line.

Will you take the first step?

Stay committed and focused on awareness and keep crossing the blue line.

I hear from many people about how they tried to meditate, do yoga, journal, sit quietly, or think positively, but it just did not work for them. These resources have tremendous value, but the people who participate consistently seem to get the most value. I do recommend these resources for deeper connection, but if they are not for you, they are not for you. Just keep exploring and uncovering your secret sauce. There are infinite ways for you to be more mindful.

Mindfulness is a lifestyle, not a here-or-there activity. Mindfulness requires consistency.

Your common sixth sense tools require consistency as well. They are readily available to you. You do not have to book a class, schedule a time, or bring supplies.

All you need is awareness of a jolt and a willingness to cross the blue line.

- Use your breath
- Manage your jolts
- Cross the blue line
- Trust your intuition
- Have awareness

You do not need to purchase a membership to use these. You came with a free, unlimited, lifetime membership.

Most people are not awake.

Wake up!

Awareness is the best caffeine you will ever consume.

WALK, DON'T RUN

Stop running toward everything.

Slow down, detach, and attract. Let it meet you halfway. Trust. What you seek is also seeking you.

Lean on your spiritual support team. Save some of your energy.

All you must do is remember to breathe.

Just breathe.

SPIRITUAL SUFFOCATION

Sometimes, spirituality is overwhelming and suffocating. Trying to be aware all the time and making conscious, purposeful decisions can get the best of us if we let it. It's important to maintain a healthy balance of awareness, yoga, meditation, consciousness, juice cleanses, breath work, journaling, deep conversations, appreciation, rising above the noise, observing, listening, staying present, making time for yourself, intentional eating, practicing gratitude, and letting go. Ugh! This is exhausting.

When people have spiritual overload, they will:

1. Walk away, sometimes indefinitely.
2. Plateau.
3. Experience increased stress/anxiety.

Spirituality and mindfulness are meant to enhance your life. If all of this feels like it is starting to lose its luster, or if it feels contradictory, something is off. Regroup and modify. You do not have to be superhuman. Try your best to maintain the balance; however, if it all feels like too much, take a break. After all, it does take energy to take exceptional care of yourself.

Listen to the four internal voices (your mind, heart, body, and gut) and make sure the messaging is in alignment with your authenticity. Be extra cautious about the messaging from external influences (the fifth voice).

Take the day off. You can be more mindful and spiritual tomorrow.

What matters is what you make matter. In other words, where your energy goes, so it goes. You can make anything or anyone matter, depending on the amount of energy you exert on that person or thing.

Sometimes, you just need a break from it all.

When someone takes a big, deep breath, instead of asking, "What's wrong?" consider what might be right.

VIBES

My life adventure so far spans five states. Saying goodbye to the majestic Rocky Mountains of Colorado meant saying hello to the vibrant, white, sandy beaches of Florida. Adapting to each new, unique location required an energy adjustment period. Navigating new cultures, demographics, and the sometimes-daunting quest of identifying people who enhance my life with their energy vibe was always an experience. Each time I discovered a new person I authentically connected with, it truly was a celebratory moment. You know that feeling when someone just gets you, and you get them? Your energy aligns. There is nothing quite like it.

What type of people do you want to surround yourself with? Are you proactively doing so? Who are you surrounding yourself with? How does this affect your energy? Is it in alignment with your energy vibe?

The better you can understand your own energy, the more quickly you can identify the right people (energy) for you. You make this discovery through self-connection, by understanding the authentic you better.

We interact with many people, including friends, family members, coworkers, and those we meet while out in public, and they may or may not be compatible energies for us. Some of our struggle comes from the energy exchanges we encounter daily as we teeter back and forth, feeling connection or disconnection based on who we interact with each day.

Toxic, abusive, or unhealthy influences do not belong in your life. I do not care if they are a longtime friend or a family member; they do not deserve your energy. Give attention to your health first. You can revisit relationships later in your life. For now, it is about you and creating the peace and connection you need.

Your energy tribe should consist of people you decide to give your energy to. So, who are you giving energy to? Do you feel healthy or unhealthy, giving your energy away to them?

When we think of people we do not vibe with, we must become aware of how much energy we exert simply because we do not vibe.

So, what if we do not vibe? There are eight billion people in the world. We are going to vibe with some and not with others.

Some people think *If they are not for me, they must be against me*. This way of thinking steals energy from us. The focus is on the wrong energy space. People who fall into this energy trap become focused on the confusion they may feel. They may even become personally offended, angry, or obsessive, or they may view the other person as a hostile enemy, repetitively talking about them, thinking about them, and wasting exorbitant amounts of energy on the disconnect. Can you relate to this? People do this all the time.

What if we could free ourselves from this way of thinking? To do so, we must shift our mindset. Sometimes, we just do not vibe; we listen to two different songs. If you do not like their song, only listen to your song and turn it up.

Stay focused on putting energy into people that you do vibe with and strengthen those relationships. Let go of the idea that simply crossing paths with a person, in life, means you should listen to the same song.

Look out for people who antagonize you and your energy. They know you do not vibe with them and want to see how much of your energy they can steal.

You are too smart for that. You have common sixth sense now.

Allow the ebb and flow of connection and disconnection.

CALM DOWN

Everybody benefits from you being a calm energy.

Having a calmer state of mind helps you navigate life stressors and the unexpected twists and turns you encounter daily.

People who are consistently calm are more approachable, understanding, and compassionate.

You are a human being, and you have every right to feel irritated, angry, or even furious. However, you should generally strive to be calm.

Calmness is a magnetic energy. The more centered you become, the calmer you become. A calm person is the voice of reason. A calm person is a safe space. A calm person has energy control. A calm person can demagnetize negative energy to lessen their own suffering, and this ability impacts the effects of suffering on those around them.

If you can manage energy, you will experience calm. If you mismanage energy, you will experience chaos.

$$E = mc^2$$

BREATHE

All suffering exists in the space between breaths.

Just breathe.

Your breath intercepts your suffering.

CAN I GET THAT RECIPE?

Everything you resonate with, stand for, or believe in should be ingredients in your secret recipe, consciously created and executed by you, for you.

Be careful of people who want to change the ingredients or call the recipe their own.

When you feel an energy jolt, ask yourself, "Is this a crisis or an awakening?"

Sometimes, it is a crisis, but most of the time, it is an awakening.

An awakening is an opportunity for you to stay present and gain the awareness needed to make changes that support your healthiest quality of life.

CHAPTER EIGHT

THE LONGING

If you have been holding back, it is time for you to jump into the deep end.

I will hold your hand if you are scared. Come on. We will do it together.

Keep your eyes open when you jump. You will want to be fully present for this experience.

Take a breath.

We all long for the same things. Security. Happiness. Health. Belonging. Connection. Love.

Feelings of longing tend to imply that something is missing, and if we had it, we would no longer long, but even when we have what we want or need, we still experience longing.

When we long, it can mean something is wrong, but not necessarily. We still long when things are right.

What if you could strengthen your relationship with longing simply by understanding it better? This relationship is no different than any other relationship you value. The more you understand it, the more you can accept it as it is.

We are longing beings by design. Longing is a fundamental, biological, and spiritual need. Longing is natural and innate and reappears time and time again. It is that which we desire, which ebbs and flows. When we are unhealthy, we long for health. When we are healthy, we long to stay healthy. When we are unhappy, we long for happiness. When we are happy, we long to stay happy. We ache for it when we don't have it and desire not to lose it once we do.

The longing stays consistent. Accepting this reality can free you of suffering. Understanding that longing will be a consistent energy in your life is imperative, and it must be managed properly.

One way to manage longing better is to be more grateful, therefore reducing the frequency of longing.

You can try to be less idealistic, accept dissatisfaction, or think more positively, therefore reducing the intensity of the longing, but you will still long.

This does not mean you stop pursuing your most connected life; it means the opposite. Pursue your desires, needs, and goals with an awareness of longing.

Have you longed for a vacation, gone on vacation, and then longed for a different type of vacation while on vacation? Have you longed for a partner, received a partner, and then longed for a different partner? Have you longed for a career change, started a new job, and then longed for a different environment?

Try to decrease your battles with the feelings of longing. Lay down your sword and call a truce. Accept that longing will consistently appear in your life. Try to find peace with longing. It is not going anywhere, so you might as well invite it in and get to know it better.

You can certainly manage longing better with gratitude, awareness, and present-moment experiences.

What would your quality of life be like if you could cross the blue line and unleash your connected, authentic self? I mean, really unleash it.

What does that even look like for you? Imagine your life, just more authentic and connected.

What if you stopped holding back and got to experience life more organically? That is what it feels like in the deep end.

To cross the blue line, you must be willing to take a risk. You must be willing to be the hero and the villain. You must be willing to let your authentic voice speak. You must be willing to do something different. You must be willing to act. You must be willing to honor your mind, body, and spirit. You must be willing to widen your lens. You must be willing to manage energy.

How can you cross the blue line right now?

Remember, awareness is one thing, but action is everything!

What is holding you back from a more authentic life?

It is not difficult; it is simple:

- You feel a jolt.
- You breathe.
- You become aware.
- You decide to cross the blue line.
- You act.
- You lessen suffering.

By no means am I suggesting your unique challenges are not difficult. What I am suggesting is that you have the absolute power to decrease suffering—one jolt, one breath, and one decision at a time.

Give yourself permission to take action to decrease your discomfort or pain. You deserve that and so much more.

The goal is to reduce suffering.

We must ask ourselves what we can individually do to reduce our suffering.

Suffering is a scale. Being too cold or too hot in your office day after day is suffering. Spending time around low-vibration people is suffering. Getting a life-altering diagnosis is suffering. Not loving yourself enough is suffering. Avoiding addressing your suffering is, in and of itself, suffering.

We suffer big, and we suffer small.

Let's do what we can daily to reduce suffering. Let's use what we already have. Let's use common sixth sense.

THE RETURN OF THE FREE SPIRIT

You deserve to feel peace. Your spirit wants peace. Your authentic self wants you to rediscover peace.

Your free spirit . . . When did you say goodbye? You must examine how and why you may have lost touch with your authentic self, accept your findings, and use that information to elevate your life.

Self-exploration reveals valuable information that can be used to your advantage as you reconnect with your free spirit.

It is okay if it feels like your free spirit has long been lost. Rest assured, it is closer than you think.

Let's look at your life:

The Freedom

Early on in your life, you may have experienced a sense of freedom or been a free spirit.

The Disruption

At some point, you may have experienced a disruption, which could have been an intense challenge or trauma. A significant jolt occurred, and it disrupted your spirit.

The Robbery

This disruption may have left you feeling disconnected, confused, on autopilot, anxious, and far removed from your authentic self.

The Survival

You then entered survival mode, living in a state of fight-or-flight, on edge, chronically worried, or overwhelmed. You felt off, like a version of yourself. You were still you, just slightly different. How long have you been functioning in this space? Are you in survival mode right now? Perhaps you are having an aha moment. I know, it sucks. I have been there, too.

The Responsibility

Your life shifted from functioning in a natural, free-spirited space to feeling a tremendous amount of heaviness and discomfort while the alarms of your mind, body, and spirit repetitively sounded.

This is not how you are meant to experience your life. Chronic stress impairs connection, and you are innately designed for connection.

How do we reclaim our free spirit?

We start with awareness. We must have the will to reclaim it and believe that our comeback will be greater than our setback.

Free-spiritedness is not free. It is a collaboration between you and your authentic self. It is an agreement you make with yourself—every day, someday, today.

Your free spirit is always present, but it takes a conscious decision from you to release it. Will you keep it restrained or unleash it? Make the agreement. Let it out. Set it free.

Your free spirit is ruled by authenticity. You are the only one who innately knows what is authentic for you.

What voices are preventing you from connecting with your free-spiritedness? Your mind? "I might fail." Your heart? "I always have to put others before myself." Your body? "I must change to be accepted, admired, or loved." Other people? "You can't be successful doing that." Environments? "This is all you deserve." Technology? "I intimately understand you and can provide exactly what you need."

See how our free-spiritedness can get lost?

Do not worry; your free-spiritedness is ready to be found.

Have you been longing for your free spirit? It longs for you, too.

What are you going to do today to reunite with your free spirit?

We must get back to ourselves.

The energy influences in your life will try to tell you who you are. Even if they have good intentions, they do not know you like you know you.

Your intuitive voice knows you best because it is quite literally you.

Do you feel any closer to yourself than you did before you started reading this book? I hope so.

It is time to start honoring your sacred, innate gifts and leaning back into your authentic spirit for guidance.

Trust yourself.

LISTEN MORE

Many answers come from your silence.

You can reduce suffering and experience more peace. It is possible.

Your awareness and breath help you make healthier decisions, therefore reducing suffering and making space for peace.

suf·fer·ing
/ˈsəf(ə)riNG/
noun
The state of undergoing pain, distress, or hardship.

a·ware·ness
/əˈwernəs/
noun
Knowledge or perception of a situation or fact.

breath
/breTH/
noun
The air taken into or expelled from the lungs.

de·ci·sion
/dəˈsiZH(ə)n/
noun
A conclusion or resolution reached after consideration.

re·duce
/rəˈdo͞os/
verb
Make smaller or less in amount, degree, or size.

peace
/pēs/
noun
Freedom from disturbance; tranquility.

What were you like as a child? What did you naturally gravitate toward? What felt right? What felt wrong?

What if you could have healthily managed the negative energy from your childhood influences? What if you had the power as a child to create a more authentic, connected life? How much suffering would you have spared yourself from?

You did not have power or energy management skills then, but you do now.

- What if you were the parent of you?
- Would you keep you safe and healthy?
- Would you encourage you to be authentic?
- Would you love you unconditionally?
- Would you be compassionate?
- Would you provide education and tools?
- Would you instill trust and self-acceptance?

If you did not receive what you needed in childhood, you have the opportunity now to reclaim the spirit of your inner child.

You deserve to experience a more powerful and free-spirited life. You owe that to your inner child.

What would it feel like for your childhood spirit and your adult spirit to collide? You would be an unstoppable team.

Your common sixth sense is an expansion and a reconnection.

We evolve so much during our lives, yet when we reunite with our authentic self, we are the same.

What does spirituality mean to you?

Is this your truth or someone else's?

Forgiveness is freedom.

However, it is not quite that simple. Forgiveness is a process. The decision to forgive is just the beginning—the first step and the catalyst of the process.

People are surprised to experience anger, hurt, resentment, and even fury after deciding to forgive, but these energies still exist in our minds, bodies, and spirits long after the decision to forgive is made. It can take months, years, and even a lifetime for the negative energy to dissipate and dissolve completely.

I wish I had understood more about forgiveness when I first decided to forgive.

I want you to know that sometimes, forgiveness takes time. It can be slow-moving and a gradual undoing. Sometimes, we do get lucky, and forgiveness is fast. You may decide to forgive, and voilà—the suffering lifts. It's a wonderful outcome, albeit a rare one. Understanding that forgiveness is more of a process than a source of immediate gratification is a valuable insight as you navigate your journey.

Every time you find yourself confused as to why negative energy is resurfacing, remind yourself that it is just the process of forgiveness. Do not let this energy deter you. It is trying to climb its way out of your life forever, and that takes time.

When you decide to forgive, it is the beginning, not the end.

Allow yourself grace and compassion as energy resurfaces over time. Remain hopeful because you are getting closer to the moment when you realize the negative energy is long gone, far removed from your mind, body, and spirit forever.

It is worth the wait, I promise.

Forgiveness is a process of freedom. This process helps return you to your free spirit.

UNDO IT

What story do you want to finally, once and for all, let go of?

Make the decision. Take action. Undo it.

It does not serve you any longer, and you know it. Say goodbye and imagine it unraveling, unwinding, and invalidating itself right out of your life.

Any story you tell yourself is revocable at any time.

It's like believing the deep end can only offer panic, but after jumping in, you discover peace.

How can you begin to undo a story using your common sixth sense?

The best part about the deep end of a pool is that it is deep.

You won't ever want to waste your energy in the shallow end again.

CHAPTER NINE

THE WAVE

Waves are energy. Waves are jolts. Jolts are energy.

How do you respond to jolts? How do you respond to waves? What is your strategy?

Take the hit.

- Do you quickly lose your balance and passively take the hit? Do you find yourself disoriented, perplexed, and uncomfortable? Do you get pushed to all the wrong places as you get demolished by the thrashing waves? Look out, here comes another one!

- Are you a complacent receiver of energy?

- What is happening in your mind, body, and spirit when you passively keep taking hits from the energy influences in your life?

Avoid the wave.

- Do you avoid waves by swimming away from them or by refusing to even get in the water? Are energy waves too much for you to handle? Is it better to pretend they do not even exist?

Face the wave.

- Do you face waves head-on and approach them with an energy plan? When you anticipate a wave, you can dive into it with intention and gracefully exit on the other side, unscathed. The best-case scenario is that you become so skilled at navigating waves that you get to ride the wave and experience the euphoria of connection and freedom.

- This strategy requires a proactive energy management system.

If we keep taking the hits, we lose all our power. When we avoid waves, we never get to be empowered and experience what riding a wave feels like. Face it, manage it, navigate it, and get on the other side of it so it does not have an influence over you any longer.

Stop mindlessly taking hits and avoiding waves. Your life is too meaningful to live in this low-vibration state.

How do you get to a high-vibration state? How do you face waves?

1. You must be willing. Do you want to change it?
2. You must accept responsibility. The waves are going to come whether you actively manage them or not.
3. You must commit. Have a consistent energy management plan in place.

Can you imagine your life without your intense external or internal reactions to waves? What does that feel like?

SOUL SURFERS

Have you ever heard of a soul surfer? Soul surfers are people who want to experience the euphoria of riding waves, not for competition's sake but simply to be present. They are motivated by the love of the solo sport and believe soul surfing heals the soul. They skillfully navigate waves with self-trust and intuition.

What if you approached waves like a soul surfer, with a sense of calm rather than chaos?

What if you shifted your perspective about waves, from the smaller waves that lightly roll in to the immensely powerful waves that come crashing down on your life? What if you perceived waves through a wider lens?

The waves are not your enemy. The waves simply exist. We vilify the waves, assuming they exist to throw us off-balance, ruin our day, or strike us to the core of our being, but they are nothing except the energy we assign to them.

These waves are notifications, awakenings, and they offer us valuable information that helps uncover our energy skill set or lack thereof.

Life is much calmer with an energy management system in place.

You deserve to experience life as a soul surfer. You deserve calm in your life.

Are you willing? Do you accept responsibility? Are you committed?

The waves are going to keep coming, but it is up to you to navigate them.

HOW DO WE FACE THE WAVES?

Use your tools.

$$E = mc^2$$

Energy = *My* management or mismanagement = *My* chaos or *My* calm.

- Breath
- Jolt to action
- The blue line
- Awareness
- Intuition

When we face the waves, we do not end them; there will always be waves. However, we decrease the energy impact they have on us.

Take action that supports your most connected life so you can spare yourself the exhaustion of battling waves and get closer to the euphoria of soul surfing.

Every time you get jolted, ask yourself, "Is this a wave I want to battle or a wave I want to ride? What can I do to decrease the size of this wave?"

Facing a wave is a choice. Do you want to get on the other side of the blue line?

The power is yours and always has been. Manage your energy and manage your life.

Every wave you face is an opportunity to cross the blue line and widen your lens.

Taking hits and avoidance hurts your spirit.

What about the spirits of those around us? Our lack of navigational skills hurts our loved ones' spirits.

The ultimate wave to face is the intergenerational wave. It's like navigating and riding the biggest waves ever surfed, in the Praia do Norte in Nazaré, Portugal. Can you imagine the feeling a surfer would experience from accomplishing this feat?

Now, imagine your intergenerational entanglements. What inherited sea debris are you intertwined with? What intergenerational traumas are you battling? What unwanted familial patterns are you repeating? Do you want to break the intergenerational wave and create a more stable energy flow for future generations?

Breaking this wave is the ultimate soul surfing. To break the wave, you must face the wave.

RUNNING ON E

The level of energy management capabilities that someone has matters.

Imagine that people have fuel tanks. Some people do not understand how to use fuel in a healthy way, often wasting fuel, running on empty, or selfishly trying to extract all your valuable fuel for themselves. Some people are limited in awareness, self-awareness, compassion, and common sense. Do you know anyone like this? Stop expecting people with low tanks to behave like they have full tanks. They do not.

See yourself and others as complex beings with varying energy abilities and fuel tank reserves. If we accept other people as complex beings with individual energy deficiencies or surpluses, we can reserve our own fuel instead of continuing to waste and deplete it on external influences that run on low tanks or try to siphon ours.

If we allow it, compassion can even surface and spare us even more suffering. Can you find compassion in people who use low tanks and run on empty? What happened in their lives to cause them to behave, think, or respond the way they do? They may be difficult to understand because they do not use the same fuel as you. Their behavior is not personal. They use their fuel their way, and you use yours another way. Your fuel is used more healthily due to your common sixth sense.

This does not excuse inappropriate or toxic behavior. You can be compassionate and set boundaries or choose to exclude people from your life altogether. If a person consistently affects your spiritual health in a negative way, you must use your fuel appropriately to make the healthiest decisions for you. You are learning how to conserve, manage, and refuel your energy. Use what you are learning and take action that supports a healthier well-being.

Have you reached out to your spiritual support team today?

What do you need?

Do not hold back. Ask. Keep working toward a deeper relationship and more consistent communication. Remember, your spiritual support team is working on your behalf, guiding and directing you, and then redirecting when you get off course. Lean on your team.

How does your team communicate with you?

Through People

- Have you ever met someone by chance? Or conversed with a person who delivered the exact information you were searching for?

Through Objects

- Have you ever been hyperfixated on an object, as if it pulled you in or presented itself to you?

Through Experiences

- Have you ever felt like an experience was divinely orchestrated?

Through Dreams

- Have you had a dream about someone who has passed away, one that felt as if it really was the person? Many people describe the experience by saying, "It felt so real!" Did this leave you curious about the spiritual world?

Through Thoughts

- Have you ever had an impactful thought enter your mind without explanation as to where it originated from? How about an epiphany? An aha moment?

Through Numbers

- Have you ever seen repetitive numbers or felt pulled toward something, only to then discover familiar and meaningful numbers?

Through Physical Sensations

- Have you ever had a gut feeling, the hairs stand up on the back of your neck, goosebumps, or a sense that your body remembers something?

Through a Knowing

- Have you ever just known something, without an explanation?

What communication have you experienced from your team? Become more aware of how hard your team is working on your behalf.

DECISIONS, DECISIONS, AND MORE DECISIONS

If you do not know what decision to make, simply make a decision. Act.

Will it be the right decision or the wrong decision?

Because we are so dependent on people, environments, and technology, we often find ourselves experiencing analysis paralysis—feeling frozen, insecure, and totally incapable of making a decision, often fearing the decision will be the wrong one. If we are able to make a decision, we experience stress and anxiety, remaining fearful that it was the wrong decision.

The truth is, we cannot know if a decision is right or wrong until we make the decision and experience the energy effects of it.

Sometimes, it is the right decision, and sometimes, it is the wrong decision. It is what it is.

How do we make better decisions? The answer is simple. Depend on yourself more. Use your common sixth sense. Stop polling your external influences to make decisions on your behalf; instead, listen to your inner voice for guidance.

When you rely more on yourself to get where you are going, you stop asking for so many directions. Use the map you came with.

Try to make one decision today using your intuition, without overanalyzing or depending on outside advice. Then observe the energy effects of this decision.

Now, do that more often.

Be conscious about the information you share with others. They may not respect and honor it the way you do. How can they, when you are the only one who can see clearly through your lens?

Take a breath.
Take a breath.
Take a breath.

Become aware of your breath.

Take a breath.
Take a breath.
Take a breath.

Where is your breath originating from?

Take a breath.
Take a breath.
Take a breath.

Relax your shoulders.

Take a breath.
Take a breath.
Take a breath.

Relax the space between your eyes.

Take a breath.
Take a breath.
Take a breath.

Relax your jaw.

Take a breath.
Take a breath.
Take a breath.

Continue reading.

You do better for the world when you operate from a calm, connected, authentic space.

When you are calm, your heart rate and blood pressure go down, your decision-making improves, your relationships strengthen, and you reduce stress.

Everyone benefits from you having an energy management system, especially you. The world needs a calmer version of you. Your mind, body, and spirit need a calmer version of you, too.

It is time to access your common sixth sense skills.

Take some time to reflect and answer the questions that follow.

What negative energy do you want to release today?

What positive energy do you want to invite in?

Is your story the same today as it was when you started reading this book? Are you sensing a shift?

Reminder: You can change the story at any time.

What waves are you battling?

What waves are you riding?

What waves are you avoiding?

What waves can you proactively prepare for and manage better?

You have the power, always. Turn around and face the wave. Your quality of life will be so much better riding the wave than battling or avoiding it.

CHAPTER TEN

THE CHOICE

Have you been crossing the blue line?

If not, now is the time. It is time to start applying concepts, being more mindful, discovering the perfect ingredients for your secret sauce, using your breath, taking conscious, connected action, living more authentically, and taking better care of yourself.

Remember, the blue line is your decision-making tool. It is available to you when you receive jolts, get hit by waves, or encounter energy vampires. The blue line is always accessible to you.

The question you must ask yourself to cross the blue line is, "What action can I take to get closer to my most authentic and connected life?" Then, you act!

The blue line is always available to you, not just for navigating life's negative energy but for navigating all of life's energy. It does not discriminate. The blue line is available to inspire you, energize you, help you take healthy risks, and encourage you to live your life with authenticity and love. It supports you through the positive, negative, and mundane moments.

Any time you receive a jolt or need guidance in making the best decision possible for you, envision the blue line. Remind yourself that you have absolute energy power.

You now have common sixth sense tools to help you navigate life from a more connected space. Are you going to experience life in a reactive energy state or a connected energy state? You must make the decision. Hint: Use the blue line to guide you to your healthiest decision.

Do you want a life where you mindlessly react to energy jolts, allowing the fuel in your spirit to continuously deplete? Or do you want to live a life where you have energy freedom and make conscious, connected, self-care decisions, all while maintaining premium fuel in your tank?

Your tank is not going to fill itself. You must do it for you. The choice is yours to make.

The breath adds fuel to your tank. Awareness adds fuel to your tank. Self-awareness adds even more. Action fills it up.

CHOICES

Your most connected life is a choice.

Lean on *you* more when making choices.

It is beneficial to consider the advice and guidance of others *if* you can separate their voices from your own.

Choose the voices you rely on in your life wisely. People can only offer information from their own lenses of life. What size lenses do the influences you seek guidance from have? I hope they are wide lenses. What are their intentions? Are the intentions right for you? Everyone has an agenda based on their life lens. Their agenda can add value to your life, but it can also mislead you. Be mindful of agendas and intentions.

Intentions are the backbone of choices. Consider your own intentions when making choices. If your intentions are well-meaning, you can find more peace in the energy results or repercussions of your choices.

If a particular choice did not land in the way you anticipated, reflect on it and do better next time. Your common sixth sense skills will get sharper either way. If you are a proactive participant in your choices, you are growing, evolving, and learning how to make healthier choices that benefit you, others, and the world.

We all make bad choices sometimes, even with good intentions. So much of life is trial and error. Always have good intentions so that when you put yourself on trial, you can find compassion in your errors.

If you have made unhealthy decisions in the past due to a more limited life lens, learn and grow, but do not give yourself a life sentence for only knowing what you did at a particular time in your life. We make decisions based on our energy capabilities at each given moment of our lives.

Hold yourself accountable for creating your most authentic and connected life moving forward. You have more common sixth sense now, so you can make healthier decisions.

People with bad intentions . . . well, that's an energy job for karma to deal with. Don't make it your life's work.

Make well-meaning decisions, keep widening your lens, and move on with creating an exceptional life. You have an incredible life ahead of you, regardless of the choices you have made in the past. Find compassion in your past decisions, have good intentions, widen your lens, keep evolving, and keep crossing the blue line.

Remember, mindfulness is a preventative tool. Use it for support when making the best possible decisions for yourself moving forward.

How are you choosing to respond to the tidal waves from energy influences today?

Our dependency on external influences is crushing our spirit.

Can you separate their voices from your own? How often are you adjusting your soul's voice for others? How often are you silencing your own voice and allowing less qualified voices to dominate your life, your perception of self, and the decisions you make?

Awareness = Self-Awareness

Continue to identify and manage the voices of your influences, and they will not have as much influence over you.

Ask someone who knows you best—you.

Common sixth sense is about taking a step back
so you can leap forward.

We must be still, observant, aware, reflective, intuitive, and
compassionate to cross the blue line. The more we do this, the easier
it gets to elevate our lives. Making decisions that best support our
well-being becomes more organic and authentic.

You have the right to protect your energy. One of the most loving steps you can take for yourself is to create distance from external influences.

The most loving thing you can do for yourself is to shorten the distance between you and your soul's voice.

SPIRITUAL OBSTACLES

Are you feeling more aligned with your spirit? If not, you may be facing some of the following obstacles as you reconnect and realign.

Restlessness

It may feel foreign to slow down. Think of your connection with yourself like having coffee with an old friend. You may be excited to become reacquainted, but you may also feel nervous or unsettled because a lot of time has passed, and now the caffeine is kicking in. Oh boy! In moments of self-connection, push through the restlessness. Spiritual exploration is like meeting up with an old, familiar friend. Once you settle in a bit, everything flows comfortably and naturally. There is so much peace waiting for you on the other side of your restlessness.

Loneliness

Not everybody dives this deep into self-exploration. You may feel like jumping back into your typical life because it is familiar and most comfortable—but that does not mean it is healthy, authentic, or connected. Resist the urge to abandon your exploration for momentary comfort. Sometimes, self-exploration can feel lonely because the people or systems you encounter are no longer serving you the way they did before. This awareness is growth, and sometimes, growing feels isolating. Remind yourself that more authentic connections are around the corner.

Polarization

The pressure to align yourself with a group or a specific mindset is a challenge we all face in today's landscape. Remember, your spirituality is uniquely yours. Be mindful of who and what you choose to align yourself with and make sure the decision is yours alone. Stay strong when pressured to think or act in any way that does not resonate. You move too far away from yourself when you mindlessly accept influencer voices to fit in or when you cave to the pressure of picking a side.

Pride

Do you need to be right, or do you want to feel peace in your body, mind, and spirit? Self-awareness is not without humbling moments. Don't let your pride detour you when your ego gets bruised.

Anger or Frustration

Anger is big-time energy. Many people give up when they become angry or frustrated. You are allowed to feel angry and frustrated. Experience the powerful energy charge that comes along with anger, but do not give these emotions the ultimate decision-making power. Find ways to regroup when faced with these emotions. Consider better self-care strategies to avoid entrapment in the suffering spiral of anger and frustration. Just because something fires you up does not mean you should abandon it.

Resisting the Surrender

When you let go and accept the messages from your body and spirit, you will learn. This can be a vulnerable experience and requires surrender. If you resist surrendering during teachable moments, it may hold you back.

Lack of Willingness to Let Go of the Story

What would life be like if you could unload some of your unhealthy attachments to people, thoughts, and behaviors? Are you willing? Deeper spiritual connection will mean writing new stories, but these will not be like essays you were forced to write in high school—they will be more like screenplays for Academy Award–winning films.

You Stop Having Fun

Self-exploration can be exciting, invigorating, and fulfilling. You are allowed to have fun on this journey. Just because something is deep, has layers, or can be difficult does not mean you cannot experience or create enjoyment out of it. The stronger your connection with your spirit, the more clearly you understand exactly what is needed for your joy and fulfillment. Go toward what you naturally connect with and have some fun along the way. The path to spiritual connection leads to energy freedom.

Skill
/skil/
noun
The ability to do something well.

Your common sixth sense skills are an asset in your life. They help you navigate your life well. I would imagine you desire to navigate life well.

Applying your skill set will improve your navigation skills. You want to become highly skilled at understanding yourself. You want to become highly skilled at understanding energy. You want to become highly skilled at creating connections that enhance your life.

What skills are you developing?

- Breathing
- Cultivating awareness
- Deepening self-awareness
- Responding to energy jolts
- Taking purposeful, connected action
- Building self-trust
- Listening
- Identifying the voices of external influences
- Crossing the blue line

These common sixth sense skills are valuable resources when it comes to problem-solving and life management.

You have skills; use them. Your skills are an asset in your life. You must keep your skills sharp. Your skills can only get sharper from here.

EMPOWER TRIP

You have been working hard. I think it's about time for an empower trip.

All the energy information you have been gathering and processing is hard work, and you are producing powerful results. That is a lot of energy!

As you elevate your awareness, adjust, and make healthier decisions in your life, you experience empowerment. It feels so good to honor your spirit. This empowerment is rightfully yours. You can claim it as your own, and it will never be taken away from you, unless you allow it to be.

This is not about having power over others, being above anyone else, or being more masterful than the narrow-lens thinkers; it is about you, your growth, your commitment, your will. It is about your body and sparing yourself from the repercussions of reacting. It is about your mind and proactively quieting those messages that no longer serve you. It is about your heart and understanding that well-meaning intentions are not always the right answer for you. It is about your spirit and reclaiming the relationship with yourself.

Celebrate each moment of empowerment when you cross the blue line.

You cannot cross the blue line unless you have made a proactive decision originating from a state of self-connection and authenticity.

Bravo! You have honored your mind, body, and spirit. Each time you do this, you should be proud. Celebrate your courage and revel in the perks and rewards your empower trip brings into your life.

BE AWARE OF ARTIFICIAL INGREDIENTS

You will naturally gravitate toward more organic and authentic people, environments, and technology as you build your recipe for a more connected life.

Use your intuition and cultivate your inner voice to make more connected decisions. What feels natural? What feels artificial?

Let's consider artificial intelligence (AI). AI is a powerful external influence in our lives. AI is not innate. AI is not spiritual. AI is not a substitute for your mind, body, or spirit. AI does not know you better than you know yourself. Be cautious of how much energy you exert on and absorb from AI.

Let's go straight to the source to find out how powerful this influence is. I used ChatGPT to uncover the answer. This next excerpt is copied directly from a ChatGPT prompt and is not edited.

Prompt:
What effect will AI have on the human spirit?

ChatGPT response:
The effect of artificial intelligence (AI) on the human spirit is a profound and multifaceted question, blending technology, philosophy, and spirituality. While it's difficult to predict the full scope of this impact, several potential effects can be considered, both positive and challenging. Here are some thoughts on how AI might interact with the human spirit:

1. Enhancement of Human Potential

- Increased Self-Awareness and Personal Growth: AI has the potential to aid in self-discovery and personal growth, which are key aspects of the human spirit. For instance, AI-powered tools can help individuals with meditation, mindfulness, or therapy, guiding them to become more self-aware and fostering spiritual and emotional growth.

- Access to Spiritual Knowledge: AI can offer vast amounts of spiritual teachings, philosophies, and wisdom from around the world, making it easier for people to learn about different spiritual traditions. This could lead to an expanded sense of interconnectedness, helping people feel more spiritually attuned to a global community.

- Personalized Spiritual Practices: AI could potentially tailor spiritual practices (such as meditation or mindfulness exercises) to suit individual needs, helping people deepen their connection with themselves and their spiritual beliefs.

2. Challenges to Human Connection and Authenticity

- Loss of Authentic Human Connection: The human spirit thrives on deep, meaningful connections with others. As AI becomes more integrated into social interactions (via chatbots, virtual assistants, or even AI-driven relationships), there may be a risk of reduced authentic human connection. If AI begins to simulate human relationships too well, people might rely on these simulated interactions, which could potentially stifle the true spirit of emotional connection, empathy, and love that comes from human-to-human bonding.

- Overreliance on Technology: If people rely too heavily on AI for spiritual or emotional support, it could risk diminishing their own inner strength and connection to their higher self. AI, while useful, can't replace the depth of human intuition, soul work, or the complex nature of human emotion. Overdependence on external technology could prevent people from developing or nurturing their own spiritual practices.

3. Shifts in Consciousness and Identity

- Blurred Boundaries Between Human and Machine: As AI progresses, questions about consciousness and the nature of the self may arise. If AI reaches a level where it can mimic or even enhance aspects of human consciousness, it could challenge our current understanding of the human spirit. Questions of what it means to be human, whether AI could ever possess a "soul," and how AI might interact with human spirituality could become important discussions in the spiritual community.

- Identity Crisis: As AI and automation continue to evolve, humans may grapple with a shift in identity—particularly in the context of work, purpose, and meaning. If AI takes over many jobs and tasks, people may question their sense of purpose, which is intrinsically tied to the human spirit. This existential challenge could lead to a reevaluation of life's meaning, pushing people to seek deeper spiritual connections and understanding of their true essence.

4. Ethical and Moral Considerations

- Ethical Dilemmas: AI's influence on the human spirit might lead to ethical dilemmas related to the use of AI in spiritual practices, healthcare, and personal development. For example, AI-driven spiritual guides or therapists might offer valuable support, but they might also raise concerns about privacy, bias, and the authenticity of the guidance provided. How can we trust AI with our most personal thoughts and feelings? The question of ethics in AI development and how it impacts human dignity and spiritual integrity is crucial.

- Moral Impact: If AI is used to manipulate human behavior (e.g., via algorithms in social media or advertising), it could challenge human free will and the integrity of the spirit. Over time, this might lead to concerns over how AI might influence or control individuals' thoughts, actions, or even spiritual beliefs, leading to a loss of autonomy.

5. Potential for Increased Spiritual Exploration

- AI as a Tool for Spiritual Exploration: While AI might not possess a soul, it could assist in guiding individuals on their spiritual journeys. AI could help map out practices, recommend spiritual books, offer personalized teachings, or even connect individuals with like-minded communities. This could serve as a helpful resource for those seeking deeper meaning, offering new avenues for spiritual exploration that might not have been accessible before.

- AI and Collective Consciousness: AI has the potential to act as a bridge to a larger, more collective human consciousness. It might help us better understand interconnectedness, both spiritually and socially, by facilitating shared knowledge and global communication. Through AI, humans might be able to connect with others who share similar spiritual aspirations, fostering a sense of unity and collective spirit.

6. A Deepening of the Need for Authentic Spirituality

- Reaffirming the Soul's Journey: As AI becomes a more significant part of our lives, the human desire for meaning and purpose may intensify. People might turn more deeply inward or to spiritual traditions to seek authenticity, connection, and wisdom that AI cannot replicate. In this sense, AI could push humans toward deeper spiritual questions, leading to greater exploration of the soul and the nature of consciousness.

- The Importance of Human Spirit in the Age of AI: With AI challenging many traditional human roles and abilities, people might feel a renewed focus on what makes humans unique—

our creativity, love, intuition, and spirituality. This could create a renaissance of spiritual exploration, focusing on the qualities that AI cannot emulate, such as compassion, kindness, and the ability to experience joy, grief, and love in deeply human ways.

Conclusion:

The impact of AI on the human spirit will likely be complex and multifaceted. While AI can provide new tools for spiritual growth, self-discovery, and connection, it also raises ethical questions and potential threats to authentic human connection and personal autonomy. Ultimately, AI might challenge humans to redefine and deepen their spiritual practices, reaffirming what it means to be human in a world where technology plays an ever-increasing role. Whether AI enhances or detracts from the human spirit will depend on how it is integrated into society and how humanity continues to value and cultivate its inner, spiritual life.

I hope for humanity's sake that we choose to value and cultivate our inner spiritual lives.

AI is not unlike any other influence; it has its own agenda, and that is to think on your behalf.

"I THINK, THEREFORE I AM."
— RENÉ DESCARTES

Make sure you think for yourself.

You can manage any agenda of any influence if you maintain a strong sense of self, use common sixth sense skills, and prioritize your innate abilities.

Let your intuitive voice lead and contemplate the ways your innate voice can collaborate with AI in healthy, productive, and balanced ways.

Consider yourself warned. AI is a transformative external influence that may have a significant impact on your spiritual well-being if you are not smarter than the system. Be smarter than the system.

You have the right to decide who you share your energy with. It is your choice.

Everything is a choice. Your energy management will define your choices.

Remember, energy is positive, energy is negative, energy is neutral.

The more you can hover in neutrality, the better your energy management system is. If you were thinking positive energy is the best energy, you may be surprised to learn that neutral energy is the preferred energy. Why? It is the most well-managed energy state because it is the most stable. Stability is healthy, balanced, trusted, steady, secure, and not likely to fall apart or deteriorate.

You are the greatest source of stability in your life. Choose stability. Choose people, environments, and technology strategically. Choose your energy encounters mindfully. Choose to listen to your intuitive voice. Choose to manage energy. Choose to cross the blue line.

Pay more attention to your everyday choices and how they affect your energy. You do not always need to make the right choice; just make the best choice with the best intentions.

Do not give external influences the power to bring you up or down, make you happy or sad, or stabilize or destabilize your energy. Most importantly, never give external influences the absolute power to determine your overall quality of life. If you are letting them do so, it is because you are letting them do so.

You decide. You hold the power. The choice is yours.

VIP STATUS

No matter what advice you receive—even from this book—it is always your choice whether to accept or decline it. Even when unwanted advice crashes your party (because sometimes it does), you always have the right to have it removed.

When it comes to your own intuition, you can choose to accept the advice or ignore it completely, but I do not recommend the latter. Trust the advice of your intuition.

Your intuition is the VIP of all energy advisors. Why do you roll out the red carpet for external voices when they are not the distinguished guest? You are.

Often, we ignore our intuition, choosing instead to honor the voices outside of ourselves.

Intuition is not confusing. Intuition is clear. Intuition has the best intentions.

I hope you will thank your intuition when receiving your lifetime achievement award.

MINDFUL MICRO-ACTIONS

Start small.

Mindful micro-actions are small, intentional behaviors that help you stay present and manage stress more effectively. Unlike some traditional mindfulness practices (yoga, meditation) that can require dedicated time blocks, these micro-actions benefit your daily life with less time commitment.

Forty-three percent of our daily behaviors are habitual (Wood, Quinn & Kashy, 2002).

Mindfulness practices can reduce cortisol levels. Reduced cortisol levels contribute to better stress management and more positive health outcomes (Wilding, Prudenzi & O'Connor, 2023).

How do we incorporate mindful micro-actions into our lives?

1. Conscious Breathing
Your breath serves as a natural reset button for your nervous system. When feeling overwhelmed, practice conscious breathing by:

- Taking three deep breaths.
- Focusing on the sensation of air moving through your body.
- Allowing your breath to naturally slow down.

2. Energy Management Response
Take ownership of your energy levels by:

- Recognizing personal energy triggers.
- Acknowledging your emotional, physical, and spiritual state.
- Choosing a connected, conscious response rather than reacting automatically.

3. Intentional Daily Planning

Start each day with purpose by:

- Setting a clear intention for the day.

- Identifying potential stress points.

- Planning energy recharge breaks.

4. Strategic Energy Breaks

Incorporate mini-breaks throughout your day by:

- Taking short stretching sessions.

- Staying energized with quality food and hydration.

- Going for brief walks to reset your energy—get the energy out!

5. Present-Moment Practice

Dedicate five minutes daily to simply being present by:

- Finding a quiet space.

- Sitting without an agenda.

- Noticing your thoughts without judgment.

6. Boundary Setting

Establish clear energy boundaries by:

- Setting time limits for worry sessions.

- Creating specific timeframes for challenging tasks.

- Honoring your personal space needs.

7. Audio Energy Reset

Use sound to influence your energy state by:

- Listening to classical music.

- Exploring delta wave recordings.

- Practicing guided meditation for five to ten minutes.

8. Mindful Connection

Enhance present-moment awareness through:

- Maintaining longer eye contact in conversations.

- Practicing active listening.

- Engaging fully in personal interactions.

9. Physical Tension Release

Practice body awareness by:

- Scanning for areas of tension.

- Consciously relaxing tight muscles.

Build your energy reserves through micro-actions. Implement mindful micro-actions and create an energy management system that prevents stress accumulation, builds resilience for major challenges, and maintains emotional balance throughout the day.

Practical Implementation Tips:

- Start with one micro-action at a time.

- Track your energy levels throughout the day.

- Adjust practices based on what works best for you.

Remember, awareness is one thing, but action is everything.

How can you integrate these practices into your daily routine? What specific energy drains could these practices help you address?

Creating a more mindful lifestyle doesn't require dramatic changes. You may already participate in micro-actions each day, such as brushing your teeth, making your bed, drinking a glass of water, saying thank you, holding a door, writing a to-do list, or checking in on a friend or family member.

Take small micro-action steps for a big impact on your quality of life. Each new step is one step over the blue line.

Your micro-actions help you change the story. They allow micro-moments to release what you cannot control. Your story can be changed at any time if you choose to change it.

"But I have obstacles." What if your obstacles are stepping stones?

"But I have no power." What if you focus on your sphere of influence? What can you control?

"But I do not have a choice." You always have a choice.

CHAPTER ELEVEN

THE CONSCIOUS REVOLUTION

THE PRIVILEGE OF A LIFETIME IS
TO BECOME WHO YOU TRULY ARE.
— CARL JUNG

So . . . who are you?

Do you understand the authentic you any better today than you did last week or last year? Are your common sixth sense abilities emerging? Is your awareness expanding?

What does your mind's voice sound like today?

What does your heart's voice sound like today?

What does your soul's voice sound like today?

I hope your voices are sounding increasingly like the authentic you. Keep growing the relationship with yourself. Find strength in understanding the authentic you.

The stronger the relationship with yourself, the less power external influence will have over you.

What are you going to do with your common sixth sense?

Why not start a revolution!

A revolution is about challenging systems and creating change. This cannot be accomplished without increasing awareness, accepting personal responsibility, and taking purposeful action.

Always challenge the system. Systems are not designed specifically for you, so you must determine how to manage your energy within the system.

Do not just mindlessly participate in systems. When we do, we either end up in exhausting energy battles with the system—confused about why it feels like such a poor fit—or we accept it without question, assuming it's right for us without ever considering if it truly is.

What systems do you want to challenge? The people in your life? Your home? Your work? Your education? The environments you encounter? The technology you encounter? The stories you tell yourself? Your overall mindset? Your relationship with yourself?

Ask yourself:

"What type of energy is working for me?"

"What type of energy is not working for me?"

These challenges create awareness. This awareness allows you to take conscious, connected, purposeful action to create your most authentic and connected life.

By challenging systems, you gain awareness. This awareness gives you valuable information that helps you make better decisions.

1. Challenge the system.
2. Gain awareness.
3. Act.

These challenges are not duels. It is not you against the world. It is simply an intuitive objection made by you, on your behalf.

The challenge comes from you recognizing that something or someone does not resonate, and the disconnect is having an energy impact on you.

The most powerful question to ask yourself is, "What am I going to do about this energy?"

The challenge is a revolution, not a rebellion. It is your awareness that something within a system does not vibe with your most authentic life. Even if it did in the past, it no longer does.

The value of the challenge is the awareness you gain. The result? Purposeful actions that more accurately represent a connected life.

Awareness = Self-awareness

Self-awareness = Better energy management

Energy-wise, you must be smarter than every system you interact with. Battling with systems takes a lot of energy, but managing them requires less.

Battling systems = Energy depletion

Managing systems = Energy conservation and replenishment

How much energy do you want to give away today?

How much energy do you want to keep for yourself?

Q & A

- How often do you notice visceral sensations in your body, like stress, muscle tightening, or jolting?

- How often are you identifying where they originate from? Inside or outside of your body?

- How often do you notice your breathing?

- How often do you feel alarms in your body?

- How often do you take action to address your energy shifts?

- How often are you engaging in activities with present-moment awareness?

- How aware are you of your thoughts and feelings?

- How often are you shifting or adjusting your energy for others?

- How often do you feel other people's energy overtake you?

- How skillful are you at managing stress?

- How often do you intentionally pause when you notice visceral sensations?

INSIDE OUT

Look inside for answers. Create your life from the inside out. Be *in*dependent. You must go in before you can go out.

The quality of your life is an inside job. That is why it is referred to as inner peace and not *outer* peace. What peace can you bring into your life today that originates from within?

Do not give your energy away for free.

Be mindful of how you distribute your energy.

THE DOORWAY

We must prepare for energy encounters. Every time you walk through a doorway, you have an opportunity to ready yourself for what comes next.

Take a breath. Roll your shoulders back. Set an intention. Open your mind. Open your heart.

Now, let your authentic spirit lead, and walk through the doorway.

No matter what or who is on the other side of the doorway, you can use your common sixth sense skills to navigate and manage the energy impact.

Do not wait for other people to recognize the authentic energy within you; show them.

GET REAL

What is your current reality?

You are the creator of your reality, and your perception creates your reality. Your perception of your life defines your life.

What reality have you created? How do you perceive your life?

You are so much more than your role as parent, student, employee, spouse, boss, volunteer, business owner, or friend.

You are so much more than your psychological or physiological challenges, like stress, anxiety, overwhelm, or chronic pain.

You are so much more than your high or low energy, agreeableness, confidence, or life-of-the-party persona.

You have a unique spirit and authentic voice aside from your interests, politics, demographics, education level, personality, behaviors, or mental health challenges. There is way more depth to you. Your depth exists inside your spirit. Your depth is the authentic you.

If you want to redefine your reality, focus more on your spirit and authentic voice and less on assigned labels.

Your spirit knows exactly who you are. Remember, you came like this.

What does your reality feel like if you strip away the labels you have assigned to yourself? What does your reality feel like if you strip away the labels other people have assigned to you? You are still the authentic you, with or without all these labels. You are simply you.

Your spirit speaks your truth. Listen.

HOMEBODY

The safest place for you to be is home.

The smartest place for you to be is home.

The most beautiful place to be is home.

The most peaceful place to be is home.

The most sacred place to be is home.

It is time to go back home.

There is no other home that is perfectly designed for you other than your own.

You have never been too far from home, although I know it feels that way sometimes.

THE ATTIC

Let's go inside your attic. (Even if you never had an attic, imagine for a moment you did.) As you climb the steps to your attic, you may notice a musty smell, and the dust may make you sneeze. It has been a while since you've been up in this attic. Go ahead and turn on the light. As you look around, you notice boxes and bins, old photos, and memorabilia. Take your time and scan the room, making note of anything that grabs your attention.

There seems to be a large piece of art that pulls you in. You may have to move a few boxes out of the way to access it, but once you do, you cannot believe what you have just discovered.

You briskly dust off the debris from the artwork, revealing a priceless, authentic piece of art. You are shocked to make this discovery. How has this priceless, authentic piece of art been hiding in this dusty old attic all this time?

You imagine all the ways your life is about to change. Now, you can start living your best life. Now, you can enjoy life the way you were meant to and the way you deserve to.

As you continue to clean off your art, something looks familiar. Wait a minute! You realize this is not a piece of art—it is a mirror, and it is your reflection you see. This is not a new discovery but a reunion. Continue to gaze into your mirror. As you look into your eyes and experience your soul, make an agreement with yourself that you will start working together as a team. Never again will you store away your most priceless possession.

It is time to leave your attic. Do not forget your mirror. Bring it with you, find the perfect spot in your home, hang it up, and look at it every day as a reminder that you already have everything you need within you.

You have *you*.

Life is much better at home.

Come back home.

Come back to you.

Of all the people I have ever known or worked with, the ones who perceive their life as good have the most peace, despite what they have experienced.

How aligned do you feel with your authentic self?

What action are you going to take to get more aligned?

Answers are not your truth. Just because someone gives you an answer does not mean it's your truth. It might be their truth, but is it your truth?

Another's voice is not your voice. The most honest voice is your authentic voice.

HAPPINESS IS PUZZLING

Happiness can be fleeting and is heavily influenced by many factors, including our biology, health, experiences, and philosophical beliefs.

Strive for peace instead. Because it originates from within, peace is a more stable state of well-being.

The problem is that most people view happiness as the goal, but even when they reach this goal, and all their "happiness" puzzle pieces seem to be in the right places, they . . . well, don't feel happy.

Go ahead and strive for that happy life, and be a happy person, but only if you can experience peace along the way.

Is your happiness dependent on the puzzle pieces fitting in all the right places? Can you experience peace when you don't have all your happiness puzzle pieces in place?

A peaceful state of mind will carry you through the missing pieces. When you finally get all the happiness puzzle pieces, you will inevitably want different pieces, a new puzzle, and so on and so forth. Humans are complicated, contentment is short-lived, and happiness goals are constantly changing or evolving anyway.

Happiness is totally overrated. Peace is totally underrated.

Strive for peace so you can have more freedom and contentment as you build your puzzle.

You have learned about waves and the tremendous impact they can have on your life.

To get closer to your authentic and connected self, you are going to have to make waves. Your connected life is an energy revolution, which will result in shifts and change. You cannot initiate change or make a shift without energy. Energy is going to create a wave.

Do not run from the waves. Face them. Manage them. Ride them.

You are not a rebel without a cause. You are a skilled soul surfer with an action plan. A strategist. A life architect. An empowered thinker.

You are going to make waves. Start envisioning your life on the other side of the blue line.

Make peace with making waves.

Think less about forcing your reality on others and more about showing the world your authentic self.

If you do so, your reality and your authenticity will naturally collide. The outcome of the collision is favorable for you and can have an inspiring impact on others.

Reach out to your spiritual support team right now
and ask for what you need.

Please go ahead and do so now—I will patiently wait.

Continue to strengthen the relationship with your team daily.
They are already working on your behalf.

Your authentic space is special and sacred; be careful who you let in.

Your common sixth sense is expanding, so you now have more discerning taste.

PEOPLE

Think of one person who continues to impact your energy in a negative way. What is their lens of life like?

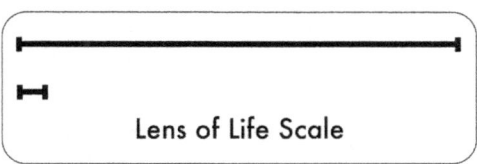

Is it wide and expansive or narrow and restricted?

What is their story? Is it a good story? Or a bad story? How much of their free-spiritedness has been stolen from their lives? What has shaped their life perspective? What is their mindset like?

Can you find compassion in their story? It will reduce your suffering if you can.

It is not your job to fix their story. They must do that work on their own. However, you can inspire them with your own actions.

THE PROJECTOR

What are you projecting out into the world?

A projector takes an image and amplifies the light to display that image on a screen.

Your light is being amplified. Wow. Think about that.

Your common sixth sense skills are emerging. Your light is getting so much brighter.

You can project whatever light you want. The power is yours. Your light, your choice. What kind of light do you want to project?

NAMASTE

— The divine **light** in me honors the divine **light** in you.

Light is a powerful energy force and a universal symbol of peace, healing, hope, faith, our inner spirit, and something greater. Light represents guidance, divinity, transformation, rebirth, and celebration.

- En**light**enment
- See the **light**
- **Light** versus dark
- Candle**light**
- Star**light**
- Sun**light**
- **Light**house
- The **light** of your soul

Are you honoring, amplifying, and projecting your **light**?

The world needs to see you.

Whatever you did or did not do, whatever you said or did not say, however you managed or mismanaged energy—you did what you could with what you knew at the time.

Now you know more. You did not know then, but now you know. Now you can make more connected, authentic decisions based on awareness and conscious, purposeful actions.

Breathe. Trust your intuition. Manage energy. Use your common sixth sense.

BACK TO THE BASICS

Common sixth sense tools are about going back to the basics.

We are getting too far removed from ourselves due to the meddling of external influences. We have given external energy permission to hijack our lives. Our passiveness has created a disconnect between dependency and independence. We need to go back to the basics and to be reminded of our innate, intuitive compass. This compass is not difficult to use. It is, in fact, simple to navigate.

We need simplified navigation skills. Your navigation system should not be overly complicated. Luckily, it is not. Navigating a spacecraft or submarine is complex. Your intuition is not; it is, in fact, the simplest navigation that exists because it requires minimal input from the user.

External influences want us to believe our own system is much more complicated than it is. This way, we must remain dependent upon them to translate it and simplify it on our behalf.

It is already simple to navigate. Do not let external influences overcomplicate your life while claiming to simplify it.

Are you ready to accept full responsibility for your quality of life?

CHAPTER TWELVE

THE BEGINNING

We experience chaos, but we deserve peace.

We must manage chaos to create our own peace.

Are you applying your common sixth sense skills in your daily life? Are you creating a connected lifestyle?

The more we incorporate common sixth sense into our lives, the more peaceful our lives can become.

So many people I have worked with or have known recognize the value in connected moments, but many feel these moments are infrequent, inconsistent, or unattainable due to the overpowering energies of life. Initially, they lack awareness of their dependency on external influences and don't understand the voices of the mind, heart, body, and spirit. The lack of awareness and the misunderstanding are the culprits that hinder connection.

How about you? Do you recognize your dependency? Do you have awareness? Do you connect with the voices of your mind, heart, body, and spirit? What energies rule your life? Are you creating connection or chaos? $E=mc^2$

How often are you using your common sixth sense to navigate energy and create your own peace? Are you enlisting support from your breath, intuition, and awareness daily? Are you taking your energy power back?

Do not depend on people, environments, or technology for peace. Your peace is independent of your external influences.

You deserve peace. You create peace. You are responsible for making peace part of your daily lifestyle, and that is empowering!

Always manage your energy first. This will save you exorbitant amounts of time interpreting, dissecting, analyzing, battling, overthinking, and wrestling with the energy of others, environments, and technology.

Keep connecting with your everyday breath.

Do not wait for moments of crisis and stress or only reserve your breath awareness for meditation- or yoga-type practices.

Use your breath as a calming, peaceful resource in moments of need and as a preventative tool to help you navigate everyday life.

Honor your relationship with your breath.

The void, the missing piece, the secret ingredient is you—
always has been, always will be.

Is your recipe coming together? Is your formula for a more
connected life evolving?

This is just the beginning of your life
on the other side of the blue line.

Slow down. Breathe. Listen to you. Trust you. Honor you.

See yourself as a separate, unique soul.

No person, environment, or technology knows your soul
better than you.

The deeper your connection to your spirit, the more
authentic your voice becomes.

Your authenticity is your most endearing quality.

The world needs more of your authenticity.

THE FORMULA

- Feel a jolt and take a breath.

- Get the energy out of your body.

- Feel the return to your body.

- Use the blue line—contemplate your more connected steps.

- Proceed with conscious, purposeful action.

- Experience connection.

If you receive a jolt and react, you experience disconnection. You may have made a calculation error. Try again next time.

Sometimes, we react to jolts even when we continuously and consciously try not to. Let it go; move on. Try again next time.

Every time you try, you gain more awareness. Never stop attempting to manage your jolts. You will lose all your power if you do.

When you accept energy responsibility, you are no longer dependent on anyone or anything.

SIM·PLIC·I·TY

/sim'plisədē/

noun

The quality or condition of being easy to understand or do.

Keep your life simple.

Energy is simple. Energy is easy to understand. You feel it in your mind, body, and spirit. It is undeniable.

Intuition is simple. Intuition is easy to understand. The soul's voice is your most trusted advisor; do not ever doubt your intuition.

Do not overcomplicate your life. Every energy jolt does not have to be explored. That would be way too complicated.

Focus on the energy jolts that have the most impact first, and as a result, the smaller jolts will not impact you nearly as much.

Seek peace in the energy you cannot understand. Find peace in the energy you do understand.

Do you feel closer to you today?

The day is not over. What can you do right now
to bring you closer to you?

At a loss? Sit with yourself for five minutes and breathe.
No agenda, just you.

YOU

I recognize and appreciate the authentic you. Even though I may not know you, I see you as a beautiful soul who aches, loves, and suffers from the inside out. The strong, resilient soul who worries, grieves, feels confused, and seeks connection. I recognize the authentic you who experiences joy, compassion, love, wonder, fear, hope, rage, and betrayal. I see you hoping and dreaming and trying to make sense of this life while seeking peace, empathy, inspiration, motivation, and laughter along the way.

If someone in your life does not have the bandwidth to understand the depths of your spirit, I will do it on their behalf, even if the person is you.

Your human existence is complex and dynamic.

Your soul's voice speaks with simplicity and clarity.

Your spirit has such a unique light. Turn up your light so we can see you better.

ROOTS

Imagine the deep roots of a tree, twisted, connected, and deeply embedded in the earth.

These roots share critical resources like water, nutrients, and sunlight.

Think about the people you are most intertwined with.

Think about the thoughts you are most intertwined with.

Think about the stories you are most intertwined with.

Now, imagine untangling and unraveling yourself from them. It is important for you to recognize that you have your own roots. Sometimes, we get so intertwined with others that we believe their roots are our roots.

Your energy is a critical resource, and you have limited critical resources to share. Always have awareness of who you share your resources with and why. Use your resources wisely.

The deep end is not scary. People do not understand their depth, so they fear it.

Use your common sixth sense to understand your depth. Be brave. Be courageous. Be fearless in your pursuit to understand you better.

The deeper you go into you, the more compassion you find for yourself and for others.

What risk are you willing to take today
to create a more connected life?

**Your common sixth sense is your energy reset button.
Press it as many times as you need.**

No matter how connected or disconnected you feel today, there is so much more peace and progress ahead of you.

You must choose to be a proactive participant in your quest for energy well-being. Choose peace. Choose progress. Choose your voice—the authentic one.

Are you strengthening your relationship with your spirit?

The growth you are experiencing and the quality-of-life improvements you are making are the result of focused and committed work.

Your lens has widened simply by reading this book.

Understand that you are establishing a new baseline for living. You cannot go backward because once you have awareness, it is yours forever. Proceed forward.

What will your next benchmark for authentic living be?

So many of our actions (or lack thereof) and thoughts hurt our spirit, and we know it.

You do not have to keep hurting your spirit. I know you want to safeguard yourself, so you hold back, play it safe, avoid, control, people-please, dismiss, overcommit, compare, self-sabotage, or deflect.

You do not have to exert so much energy trying to protect yourself anymore. Your spirit will help you find more energy freedom. Your spirit will protect you. You are an incredible team.

Effective energy management is the result of
self-awareness and skill.

Notice which parts of your body initiate your choices.

Are the choices in line with what you genuinely need, or are they simply a reaction or reflex from past experiences?

How are you reducing the energy jolts in your life?

All your actions make sense with enough information. All your reactions make sense with enough information.

Gather enough energy information to manage your energy reactions and responses.

Awareness = Information

Information = Self-Awareness

When you have enough information, you can improve your quality of life.

Live now, not later. *Now*.

A FOR EXPANSION

As you continue to gain more awareness, do not make you your project.

Having awareness and self-awareness is beneficial to your quality of life, but you are not a project that needs to be constantly graded. Learning about yourself should be a natural, organic, curious, and never-ending exploration. There is no deadline for growth and evolution. You will always get an A for expansion.

There is plenty of room in your life for self-exploration and just living life. You can do both. Be careful not to get hyperfixated on your energy management.

A balanced life includes a healthy relationship with your energy exploration.

You are a spiritual being navigating the human experience—or is it the other way around? Either way, it's complicated, and you need tools to do it well.

The goal is not to eliminate suffering—that would be impossible.

Focus on what is possible. It is possible for you to decrease negative energy impacts and reduce suffering. It is not only possible; it is probable. It is attainable.

I invite you to move from reaction to conscious response.

Do you accept the invitation to move into conscious leadership of your own life?

You must work to create your most connected and authentic life.
It won't just happen by chance.

You have the free will to shift your energy at any given moment.

Have an unstoppable drive to better manage energy and consistently cross the blue line.

You now have a clearer, more accessible framework that brings together energy management, mindfulness, awareness, self-awareness, spirituality, and personal responsibility.

You now have a perceptive ability that is far beyond "normal."

Use your common sixth sense often.

Take a big, deep breath.

Remember, you have you.

Stay in constant contact with your mind, body, and spirit. These voices communicate with you through the energy they consistently share with you.

It is your responsibility to manage their energy. Talk to them. Listen to them. Have a conversation with them, out loud or in your mind. At the very least, you must start acknowledging them for the relationship to evolve.

They are constantly communicating with you. Listen and make sure to communicate back.

A strong relationship evolves over time and from understanding and energy. Build bonds. Healthy relationships require energy—the right kind of energy.

Respect and love your voices. Have compassion for your voices. They are, after all, yours.

The people, environments, and technology you surround yourself with have a profound impact on your life. Choose wisely. Stop wasting your sacred energy on energy-depleting interactions. You are too elevated now for low vibration living.

Your life will be filled with commitments, obligations, and circumstantial responsibilities. If you choose to experience these duties with negative energy, you will suffer.

If your energy is repeatedly negative during your less desirable commitments, continue to strive for more energy-neutral experiences. Neutral energy is so much more stable than negative energy. Neutral energy will reduce your suffering. For your own sake, strive for neutrality.

If you feel substantial negative energy in your life, reconsider the people, environments, and technology you interact with.

Use your common sixth sense.

Be open to novelty.

Mindfulness is about the now. Your awareness of the now creates your new. Out with the old, and in with the new. Good riddance. Goodbye. Farewell. Warmest regards. Release with gratitude.

Say farewell and appreciate the lessons, even if they are difficult. It's time to make more room for that which serves you by releasing that which does not.

Your common sixth sense recipe will take time to create.

There will be trial and error, failures and successes, steps forward and steps back. You will inevitably burn some things along the way. Please do not stop creating your recipe for better energy management and a more connected, authentic life. If you do, you will end up going out to eat or ordering delivery, and those recipes are created by someone else.

Have you noticed that the more often you eat out or order in, the more your dining experience tends to involve unhealthy ingredients, inconsistent quality, slow service, higher costs, and food that often leaves you uninspired—while you're mindlessly consuming someone else's less thoughtful creation?

Stay focused on creating your recipe. It's going to be a common sixth sense culinary masterpiece.

You are already authentic and connected. You came like this.

It's time to unleash your most authentic and connected life and experience the energy freedom you deserve.

The more you hold back, the more you suffer.

Go far beyond normal perception. Lean into your sixth sense abilities and magnify your awareness.

Why would you ever want to experience life "normally" when you can access all of this?

Your perception is your reality. Your mindset determines your perception.

Never forget what motivates you to put the energy work in—to decrease suffering and improve your quality of life.

There is so much unlived life inside of you yearning to be set free.

You deserve to live two lives: the life you are currently experiencing and the more authentic, connected, and peaceful life that awaits you and is rightfully yours to reclaim.

Demand it.

Require it.

Declare it.

Honor it.

Feel it.

Unleash it.

Breathe it.

Live it.

Next time you dive into the deep end, make one hell of a big splash.

Our time together is coming to an end, but your deeper connection with yourself is just beginning.

It is time for you to unleash the authentic, unlived life inside of yourself, reclaim your innate, intuitive abilities, and experience your most connected life.

You can come back to Common Sixth Sense anytime you need to for guidance and a loving reminder to stay focused on your energy, spirit, and overall well-being. Read this book again and again. Contemplate the questions throughout the book. Open a random page for a quick reminder. Reread a chapter. Keep coming back.

Cross the blue line.

Ride waves.

Widen your lens.

Keep it simple.

Trust your intuition.

Take a deep breath.

Keep your eyes open.

Dive into the deep end.

Do it all with conscious, purposeful action.

It feels so good to be back home.
Welcome back to you.

~~The End.~~
The Beginning.

Take a breath. It's just a wave. You've got this.

ACKNOWLEDGMENTS

To my husband, Dave, you are an incredible best friend and life partner, and my most captive audience member. Thank you for encouraging me to go for it.

To my daughter, August, your beautiful light inspires me to be more creative, expand my mind, and make sure my words are used in the right context.

To my son, Conner, your vibrant energy brings me laughter, much-needed clarity, and the reminder to live in the moment.

To my parents, Linda and Rudy, for teaching me how to have a great sense of humor despite it all.

To my in-laws, Beth and Bill, for being such enthusiastic cheerleaders.

To my friends, for supporting my gifts and endeavors with open hearts.

To Dr. Naelys Luna, Tootie Martin, Dr. Gabriel "G" Cesar, Robin Rubin, Dr. Tony Andenoro, and the incredible faculty and students at Florida Atlantic University College of Social Work and Criminal Justice, for taking a chance on mindfulness integration. The universe brought us together, and somehow, it works.

To L.A. Perkins, for an incredible conversation during a chance meeting on a flight from Fort Lauderdale to Denver.

To Ashley Mansour, Jessica Reino, Tory Woodruff, and the team at Brands Through Books, for being consistent and encouraging voices from start to finish.

To the countless yoga instructors, meditation guides, thought leaders, spiritual educators, wellness practitioners, and psychologists who have shared your gifts—you have elevated my life.

To my clients, for sharing your most intimate, authentic, and soulful triumphs and tragedies. Your open and loving feedback encouraged me to bring my knowledge to a larger audience.

To Jill Trout, for being an awesome and insightful beta reader.

To my dogs, Fleetwood and Mac—you should be sainted for the time spent listening to my content.

To my ten-year-old self, who wrote on a piece of paper "I will write a book." I could not have done this without you.

ABOUT THE AUTHOR

Rachael Schmidt is a mindfulness-based educator and coach and the founder of Common Sixth, a lifestyle company devoted to supporting deep connection and authentic living. With over two decades of experience in spiritual development and mindful self-discovery, Rachael provides others with accessible, real-world practices that bring clarity, calm, and meaning to the complexity of the human experience.

Her work is rooted in compassion and curiosity, supporting individuals and groups—including leaders, students, and private clients—as they reconnect with their inner wisdom and navigate life with greater intention.

Rachael also serves as a community fellow at Florida Atlantic University's College of Social Work and Criminal Justice, where she offers mindfulness education and integration for faculty, undergraduates, and graduate students—bridging contemplative practice and academic and professional life.

STAY CONNECTED

Instagram: @commonsixth

Website: commonsixth.com

For **speaking engagements, consulting,** or **media inquiries**, please visit commonsixth.com.

BIBLIOGRAPHY

Brown, K. W., Creswell, J. D., & Ryan, R. M. (2025). The (further) evolution of mindfulness science. In K. W. Brown, R. M. Ryan, & J. D. Creswell (Eds.), *Handbook of Mindfulness: Theory, research, and practice (2nd ed.),* pp 9–12. The Guilford Press.

Chems-Maarif, R., Cavanagh, K., Baer, R. et al. Defining Mindfulness: A Review of Existing Definitions and Suggested Refinements. *Mindfulness* 16, 1–20 (2025). https://doi.org/10.1007/s12671-024-02507-2

Dimidjian, S., & Linehan, M. M. (2003). Defining an Agenda for Future Research on The Clinical Application of Mindfulness Practice. *Clinical Psychology: Science and Practice,* 10(2), 166–171. https://doi.org/10.1093/clipsy.bpg019

Eisenlohr-Moul, T., Peters, J. R., & Baer, R. A. (2015). How do mindfulness-based interventions work? Strategies for studying mechanisms of change in clinical research. In B. D. Ostafin, M. D. Robinson, & B. P. Meier (Eds.), *Handbook of Mindfulness and Self-Regulation* (pp. 155–170). Springer Science + Business Media. https://doi.org/10.1007/978-1-4939-2263-5_12

Generational Trauma:13+ Effective Ways to Break the Cycle. (2022, October, 22). Sandstone Care. Retrieved March 28, 2025, from https://www.sandstonecare.com/blog/generational-trauma/\

Gunsilius, C. Z., et al. Paying Attention to Attention: A Program Evaluation of Faculty-Delivered Mindfulness-Based Attention Training to Optimize Wellness and Professionalism in Medical Students. *BMC Med Educ* 24, 182 (2024). https://doi.org/10.1186/s12909-024-05119-5

Kabat-Zinn, J. Mindfulness. *Mindfulness.* 6, 1481–1483 (2015) https://doi.org/10.1007/s12671-015-0456-x

Langer, E. Matters of mind: Mindfulness/Mindlessness in Perspective. *Consciousness and Cognition. Science Direct.* Received 29 June 1991 https://www.sciencedirect.com/science/article/abs/pii/105381009290066J?via%3Dihub

Lee, C. (2024, May 23). *Newly Discovered Planet May Be Able to Support Human Life.* Time. https://time.com/6981897/newly-discovered-planet-gliese12b-life/

Madureira Pinto, L. (n.d.). *12 Signs You're a Soul Surfer.* Surfer Today. https://www.surfertoday.com/surfing/signs-you-are-a-soul-surfer

Neff, Kristin & Germer, Christopher. (2013). A Pilot Study and Randomized Controlled Trial of the Mindful Self-Compassion Program. *Journal of Clinical Psychology.* 69. 10.1002/jclp.21923.

Stephen, M. J. (2021, March 9). 2020: *The Year We Lost Our Breath*. American Lung Association. https://www.lung.org/blog/2020-breath

Tix, A. (2024, June 3). *Longing for More How the German concept of Sehnsucht sheds light on the human quest.* Psychology Today. https://www.psychologytoday.com/us/blog/the-pursuit-of-peace/201709/longing-for-more

Treves, I. N., et al. (2025). Connectome Predictive Modeling of Trait Mindfulness. *Human Brain Mapping*, 46(1), e70123. https://doi.org/10.1002/hbm.70123

Wilding, Sarah, Prudenzi, Arianna & O'Connor, Daryl. (2023). Effectiveness of stress management interventions to change cortisol levels: a systematic review and meta-analysis. Psychoneuroendocrinology. 159. 106415. 10.1016/j. psyneuen.2023.106415.

Wood, W., Quinn, J. M., & Kashy, D. A. (2002). Habits in everyday life: Thought, emotion, and action. Journal of Personality and Social Psychology, 83(6), 1281–1297. https://doi.org/10.1037/0022-3514.83.6.1281

www.ingramcontent.com/pod-product-compliance
Lightning Source LLC
Chambersburg PA
CBHW060411130626
46555CB00005B/2026